# Meilgaard Bee

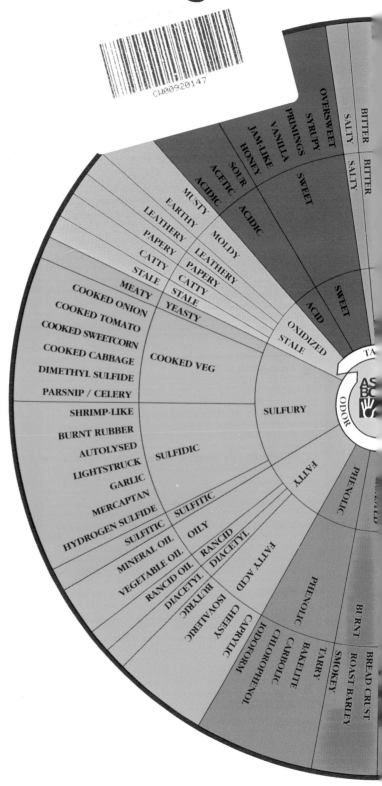

# r Flavor Wheel

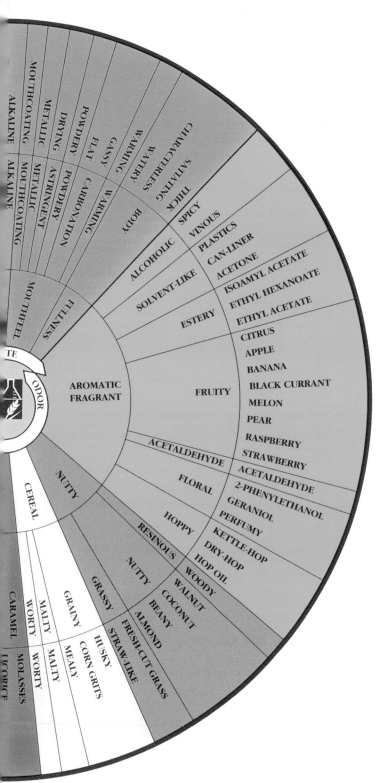

© American Society of Brewing Chemists, www.asbcnet.org/

# Beer Tasting

by Rita Kohn with Upland Brewing Company

ALPHA
A member of Penguin Group (USA) Inc.

## ALPHA BOOKS

Published by Penguin Group (USA) Inc.

Penguin Group (USA) Inc., 375 Hudson Street, New York, New York 10014, USA • Penguin Group (Canada), 90 Eglinton Avenue East, Suite 700, Toronto, Ontario M4P 2Y3, Canada (a division of Pearson Penguin Canada Inc.) • Penguin Books Ltd., 80 Strand, London WC2R 0RL, England • Penguin Ireland, 25 St. Stephen's Green, Dublin 2, Ireland (a division of Penguin Books Ltd.) • Penguin Group (Australia), 250 Camberwell Road, Camberwell, Victoria 3124, Australia (a division of Pearson Australia Group Pty. Ltd.) • Penguin Books India Pvt. Ltd., 11 Community Centre, Panchsheel Park, New Delhi—110 017, India • Penguin Group (NZ), 67 Apollo Drive, Rosedale, North Shore, Auckland 1311, New Zealand (a division of Pearson New Zealand Ltd.) • Penguin Books (South Africa) (Pty.) Ltd., 24 Sturdee Avenue, Rosebank, Johannesburg 2196, South Africa • Penguin Books Ltd., Registered Offices: 80 Strand, London WC2R 0RL, England

**Copyright © 2013 by Penguin Group (USA) Inc.**

All rights reserved. No part of this book may be reproduced, scanned, or distributed in any printed or electronic form without permission. Please do not participate in or encourage piracy of copyrighted materials in violation of the author's rights. Purchase only authorized editions. No patent liability is assumed with respect to the use of the information contained herein. Although every precaution has been taken in the preparation of this book, the publisher and author assume no responsibility for errors or omissions. Neither is any liability assumed for damages resulting from the use of information contained herein. For information, address Alpha Books, 800 East 96th Street, Indianapolis, IN 46240.

THE COMPLETE IDIOT'S GUIDE TO and Design are registered trademarks of Penguin Group (USA) Inc.

International Standard Book Number: 978-1-61564-301-1
Library of Congress Catalog Card Number: 2013930721

15   14   13        8   7   6   5   4   3   2   1

Interpretation of the printing code: The rightmost number of the first series of numbers is the year of the book's printing; the rightmost number of the second series of numbers is the number of the book's printing. For example, a printing code of 13-1 shows that the first printing occurred in 2013.

*Printed in the United States of America*

**Note:** This publication contains the opinions and ideas of its author. It is intended to provide helpful and informative material on the subject matter covered. It is sold with the understanding that the author and publisher are not engaged in rendering professional services in the book. If the reader requires personal assistance or advice, a competent professional should be consulted.

The author and publisher specifically disclaim any responsibility for any liability, loss, or risk, personal or otherwise, which is incurred as a consequence, directly or indirectly, of the use and application of any of the contents of this book.

Most Alpha books are available at special quantity discounts for bulk purchases for sales promotions, premiums, fund-raising, or educational use. Special books, or book excerpts, can also be created to fit specific needs. For details, write: Special Markets, Alpha Books, 375 Hudson Street, New York, NY 10014.

**Publisher:** *Mike Sanders*
**Executive Managing Editor:** *Billy Fields*
**Senior Acquisitions Editor:** *Brook Farling*
**Senior Development Editor:** *Christy Wagner*
**Development Editor:** *Nancy Lewis*
**Senior Production Editor:** *Janette Lynn*
**Copy Editor:** *Krista Hansing Editorial Services, Inc.*

**Cover Designer:** *William Thomas*
**Book Designers:** *William Thomas, Rebecca Batchelor*
**Indexer:** *Bradley Herriman*
**Layout:** *Brian Massey*
**Proofreader:** *Tricia Liebig*

**Cover Images:** *Sian Irvine, Kellie Walsh, Andrew Harris, Steve Gorton*

# Contents

# Appendixes

# Introduction

Everyone has a favorite story they tell and retell as a life-changing event. Recalling the ambiance, time, and place of the first Craft beer creating a "Wow!" moment is the reversal of "the big one that got away" for people who drink Craft beer.

For Anita Johnson, it was going to a pub with family in Washington, D.C., in the 1980s and asking, "Are there any local beers?" They were served Sam Adams, and they "loved it." Anita subsequently opened a homebrew supply shop.

For Ron Smith, it was while browsing the local liquor stores for the usual cheap college beer. "I would see these interesting-looking beers from around the world, and I was curious about what they tasted like." He acted on his curiosity, and he never turned back. Ron now leads beer tours to Germany and Belgium.

For Greg Christmas, it was Purdue 1982, with a "Learn how to brew beer" ad in the student newspaper. "I looked at my buddy. He looked at me. We said, 'Wow,' so we marched on down there." They tasted the instructor's brew. They said "Wow" again. Now Greg is a member of the Dogfish Head engineering/quality control team.

For Ted Miller, it was coming home from college and noticing that a brewery was open. Ted recalls, "I said to my mom, 'There's a brewery five blocks away. I'm going to work there.'" The owner told him to come back when he was 21. Ted came back, traveled the world brewing, became an advocate for Belgians and gastropubs, and opened his own gastropub specializing in Belgians.

For Cari Crowe, it was a student trip to Scotland with the discovery of beer that took her breath away. Cari now is a representative of a regional brewery with a daily mission to pair each person with the beer they will fall in love with. She says, "Getting the beer inside you and feeling the interaction when you swallow, that's a visceral experience."

And that's pretty much the point of this book—asking for what's local, getting curious about what's on the shelf from afar, going hands-on, becoming an advocate.

Acquiring a taste for Craft beer is a personal quest and a journey in partnership with others who are like-minded. Some of us are straightforward in the way we talk about our experiences with Craft beer and some of us are more effusive. What unites us is the pleasure we get from savoring a beverage linked to the human story of civilization.

*The Complete Idiot's Guide to Beer Tasting* is your personal guide to becoming and being aware of what you are drinking and eating. It's what Cari refers to as "Getting taste into your brain" in the same way that the brain can remember smells as an emotional experience.

And you've already noticed that context is of consequence—where and when, how and why, with whom and what was/is going on at that moment of discovery—a uniquely personal discovery that links every Craft beer lover to the very first brew in Ancient Mesopotamia millennia ago.

## How This Book Is Organized

Start with page one and keep going to the end, stopping along the way to join friends and family, to meet brewers and others in the brewing industry, to drink Artisan-brewed beer and eat Artisan-prepared food:

**Part 1, A Brief but Fascinating History of Beer**, takes you through the history of this frothy ferment steeped in discovery, intrigue, and return.

**Part 2, Understanding Beer**, takes you from its basic four ingredients through the art, craft, and passion of brewers.

**Part 3, The Art of Beer Tasting**, gets you hands-on with family and friends to personalize your romance with the brew that's intimately tied to just about every culture on this planet—and, for some, extends into the heavens.

Don't miss the glossary. It's your fun place to browse for those extra bits of learning beer talk.

Appendix B provides Resources to assist in your quest toward greater enjoyment of Craft beer through reading and travel.

Appendix C provides Tasting Sheets you can copy and take to tasting events. Organize them into a binder to grow your personal book of Craft beer.

## Extras

In each chapter, you'll find helpful sidebars that provide facts, tips, and extra information:

**DEFINITIONS**

These boxes give you the meaning of terms that are relevant to the topic at hand.

**BREW WATCH**

These boxes provide interesting background information that extends your basic knowledge.

**TASTING TIP**

These boxes draw special attention to beer tasting specifically.

The gift that keeps on giving through this book is your personal commitment to seeking a quality lifestyle in all you do. Craft beer is part of the human story in all its facets and phases. The story of Craft beer is interwoven with amazing events, dedicated people and the requirement that we all act responsibly. Like life itself, Craft beer is to be savored, never abused, and always respected for how alcohol in any form affects our ability to be rational.

*Salud, Proost, Prost, Prosit, Sláinte, Slainte, a votre sante, Iechyd da, L'Chaim!,* Cheers ….

And forever happily recall your special "Wow!" moments with Craft beer.

## Acknowledgments

The Craft beer industry is truly one big family. Thank you to all of you from coast to coast for answering my emails, talking to me on the phone, meeting me at festivals and tastings, and guiding me through what you all believe is essential for a newcomer to Craft brewing to become acquainted within the confines of a book.

Thank you to all the people in the industry whose stories appear in this book as part of the interwoven facets of beer.

For going the extra mile to read text and make those exacting corrections, special thanks to Bob Mack.

Utmost gratitude to owner Doug Dayhoff, brewer Caleb Staton, executive chef Seth Elgar, vice president of operations Peter Batule, brewery representative Cari Crowe, and the entire team at Upland Brewing Company who served as technical advisors.

To family and friends and medical caregivers who were with me on the incredible journey of beating cancer while writing this book, your faith is amazing.

For staying the course, appreciation to the editing staff at Alpha Books, particularly Brook Farling, for asking me to undertake the challenge.

For Andy—it would not have been done without you.

## Dedications

To Jack McAuliffe, who started the modern Craft brewery movement in 1976 with the New Albion Brewery in Sonoma, California.

To Don Barkley, who safeguarded the old brewing logs and the special yeast when New Albion closed in 1983.

To the founders of San Francisco Beer Week in 2009 for initiating "The Return of New Albion Ale."

To Jim Koch at Samuel Adams for celebrating the 80th anniversary of Repeal of Prohibition and the 35th anniversary of legalization of homebrewing with the 2013 national release of New Albion Ale as re-created by Jack and Jim.

## Trademarks

All terms mentioned in this book that are known to be or are suspected of being trademarks or service marks have been appropriately capitalized. Alpha Books and Penguin Group (USA) Inc. cannot attest to the accuracy of this information. Use of a term in this book should not be regarded as affecting the validity of any trademark or service mark.

# A Brief but Fascinating History of Beer

Beer has played and continues to play a significant role in the story of humankind. Worldwide, it is the most consumed alcoholic beverage and is third (behind water and tea) for overall liquid consumption.

We start our journey toward responsible and increasing enjoyment of Craft beer at the Cradle of Civilization some 12,000 years ago, and we travel across the centuries and continents to the present. Finding our personal place within this milieu makes us participants in the larger story of the beverage, intertwined with the making of civilization and the development of cultures.

# Early Beer Drinking Cultures

## In This Chapter

- Tracing the culture of beer
- Brewing using methods from ancient times
- Learning about beer in worldwide mythology
- Showing respect for the craft of making beer

Almost every ancient culture had myths and legends connected with beer. They recognized the nutritional value of beer even if they weren't aware of the workings of yeast, the essential factor for turning gruel into a drinkable food with nutrients beyond what grains in water impart. Thus, to our ancestors, it seemed reasonable that a deity turned a grain in a pan of water into a safe, flavorful beverage.

With no other explanation available, it made sense to believe that the people were favored (or not) by spirits that also controlled climate, weather, crops, birth, death, health, sickness, wealth, and poverty. And there's another way to see the divine in beer: ingredients from the basic universal aspects of water, earth (grains), fire (required to extract the sugars from the gains), and air (the unknown factor we now know is yeast), are all present when making beer.

This chapter takes you on a tour of the world's early cultures that believed beer was a gift from a force beyond human reckoning.

# Beer from the Fertile Crescent

We don't know exactly where, when, or by whom beer was discovered. All we have is archeological evidence that people happened upon the first brew perhaps some 12,000 years ago in the place we call the Cradle of Civilization, now known as Mesopotamia or modern-day Iraq.

Trade and exchange of ideas has been ingrained in humankind. We know from written records that beer from Babylon in Mesopotamia was on the trade route to Egypt, probably used as barter for goods from Egypt.

By 4000 B.C.E., beer was part of daily life along the Tigris and Euphrates rivers in Mesopotamia and in the neighboring Nile River Kingdom of Egypt. Together these river-based collections of communities became known as the Fertile Crescent. They became the first places people moved away from the nomadic way of life and began farming and establishing settlements.

**BREW WATCH**

Beer making preceded pottery, so the earliest brews would have been made in either closely woven baskets lined with pitch, leather pouches, or animal bladders.

## Brew Like an Egyptian

Beer became as central to everyday and religious life in Egypt as it was in Mesopotamia, and eventually Egyptian brewers developed their own way of brewing. Beer appears more frequently in Egyptian texts than any other food or beverage, and its taste and use are described in multiple ways. The Egyptians even had a separate hieroglyph for *brewer.*

Egyptian legends attribute the people's knowledge of beer making to the god Osiris. Worshiped as a god of fertility, death, and resurrection, Osiris is credited with teaching the people how to farm, thus creating civilization. Even though scholars point to evidence of Egyptian brewers making beer by mixing heated barley and *emmer* with uncooked malt and yeast, it is widely believed that early Egyptian beer predominantly was concocted from bread made from barley and water. Women made both the bread and the beer. Thus, beer became a cash commodity for Egyptian women, giving them a product they could use to barter for other goods.

 **DEFINITIONS**

**Emmer** was a wild and cultivated wheat of antiquity. Now it is a relic crop found in mountainous regions. In Italy, it is known as faro and is protected by law. Emmer has expanded nutritional qualities and can grow in poor soil and climate.

According to scholars who have studied Egyptian beer hieroglyphs, the Egyptians baked a rich, yeasty dough into a flat bread and then crumbled it into small pieces. They poured water over the bread-crumbs and then placed it in a sieve over a vat. The liquid trickled into a container, where it fermented. The brewers added dates to help in the fermentation and lend sweetness to the brew. Honey also was a likely source of fermentation because it was widely available in Egypt.

As a dietary staple for children and adults, the Egyptian brew hardly would have been alcoholic. Instead, it has been described as thick, sweet, and nutritious, supplying essential calories, vitamins, and minerals. Egyptian workers and slaves were paid in food rations of beer, fruits, nuts, and vegetables.

By the time of the Pharaohs (3050–330 B.C.E.), beer drinking had become an integral part of life for the Pharaohs as well, and they often had their own royal breweries.

Although early Egyptian writings are full of warnings against over-indulgence, myths relate instances of drunkenness especially at the Egyptian festivals to honor the main goddess of beer, Tjenenet, and the three lesser goddesses: Bast, Sekhmet, and Hathor.

## Pass It Around

The Egyptians introduced brewing to the Greeks, who called the brew Zythos, based on *zytum*, one of the Egyptian names for beer. Sophocles, who preached moderation in all things, believed beer should be part of a balanced diet that also included bread, meat, green vegetables, and fruits.

The Greeks, in turn, taught brewing to the Romans, who called their brew Cerevisia, a combination of Ceres, the goddess of agriculture, and *vis*, meaning "strength" in Latin. The Spanish assigned a similar name to beer, cerveza. And while the word *beer* has a Latin origin, it's based on *bibere*, meaning "to drink."

The Romans brought beer to northern Europe around 55 B.C.E., mostly to the Celtic tribes and the Teutnic people of central Europe. Evidence suggests Roman brewing in Kalmbach and in Regensburg, a Roman outpost that Marcus Aurelius founded in 179 C.E. as Casta Regina.

Germanic tribal people also likely were brewing in the Sumerian tradition as early as 800 B.C.E. Researchers have determined that women brewed the beer using heated fresh water and the highest-quality grains. Not until the Christian era in Germany did men learn the craft. Then monks brewed beer and sold it to support their monasteries, which served as the early prototype of hotels with rooms and food for pilgrims and other travelers. The three Christian saints known as the patrons of brewing are Saint Augustine of Hippo, author of the confessions; Saint Luke the Evangelist; and Saint Nicholas of Myra, or Santa Claus.

In another twist, Christianity's preference for wine in ritual caused beer to lose favor in early Rome, and wine replaced it as the preferred beverage of clergy and upper classes. Beer continued to be made only in the far reaches of the Roman Empire where grapes could not easily grow.

Early brewing was widespread throughout northern Europe and the Mediterranean area, and on the continents of both Asia and Africa. In his *Histories* (500 B.C.E.), Herodotus describes how the Scythians made a beer called Kumis by fermenting mare's milk. Kumis is described as having a somewhat sour flavor that varies according to who is making it.

> **BREW WATCH**
>
> In nineteenth-century southeastern Russia, health resorts served Kumis as a cure-all for whatever ailed someone. Kumis is associated with hospitality in Kyrgyzstan, where the nation's capital city, Bishkek, shares its name with the paddle used to churn the fermenting milk. In his book *A Confession*, Leo Tolstoy writes of drinking Kumis as a way to make his life bearable.

Beer is part of ancient Israelite culture. Biblical scripture contains both citations for enjoyment and injunctions against overindulgence. However, Proverbs 31:6 specifically claims that beer can be an antidote to feeling melancholy. A 2,000-year-old Assyrian tablet names beer as part of the food mainstays brought on board Noah's Ark.

Chang, a mildly intoxicating barley beer made in Tibet, is thick and white, with a sweet, pungent aroma. Chang and tea continue to be mainstays in the high, mountainous regions of Tibet, where barley itself is a food staple. As early as 23 B.C.E., the people of China brewed with millet. Called kiu, this beer played a significant part in religious rituals.

# Beer in Mythology

Beer and brewing are prominent components in the mythologies of people worldwide. In Norse mythology, Aegir, the God of the sea, also is known as the God of beer and brewing, assisted by his wife Ran and their nine daughters. They brewed *Ale* and *Mead* (fermented honey and water) for the gods.

**DEFINITIONS**

**Ale** is one of the two major types of beer; the other is Lager. Ale pre-ceded the brewing of Lager. It is fermented at high temperatures, and the yeast rises to the top. Aging takes two weeks to a month.

**Mead,** also called Honey Wine, is an ancient beverage with no known origin. It is made by fermenting honey with water and generally is the color of the honey. Some Mead makers add fruit, herbs, and *hops*; oth-ers add light malt that is strained out.

**Hops** are a flowering vine. The oil of the flowers adds flavor (bittering hops) or aroma (aroma hops). Brewers can use a single hop or a mixture to create a specific taste and aroma profile.

The head Viking god Odin cautioned against overindulgence, although Ale for Vikings was different from the Ale we know today. We talk more fully about olde Ale and Mead in Part 2. Drinking Ale was essential during seasonal religious festivals, including after the harvest, near midwinter, and at midsummer. This drinking of Ale transferred to the practice of Christianity in Scandinavia. The Gulaþing Law required farmers, in groups of at least three, to brew enough Ale for All Saints Holiday, Christmas, and the feast of St. John the Baptist. Some secular events celebrated today also are associated with beer. For example, a christening is called Barnöl (*barn* means "child") in Swedish—the word ö, for Ale, is used as a suffix here.

In Celtic mythology, Die Lati is the goddess of water and beer. Die Dagda, the Celtic god of earth, summoned the seasons with his magical harp, which is the signature symbol for Guinness beer.

Raugupatis is the god of fermentation in ancient Baltic and Slavic mythology; Raugutiene, his partner, is the goddess of beer. In Czech mythology, Radegast, the god of hospitality and mutuality, is credited with creating beer. However, Radegast's prowess has been usurped over the years: the mythical Flemish King Gambrinus, who reigned during the Middle Ages, has gained international notoriety as "the inventor of beer" and earned the (unofficial) title of Patron Saint of Beer.

**BREW WATCH**

A huge Gambrinus statue erected in Columbus, Ohio, in 1906 is still part of that city's cultural landscape, even though his namesake brewery no longer is in operation. Nevertheless, many other Gambrinus companies exist worldwide. The American Homebrewers Association annually presents the winning homebrew club the Gambrinus Award.

The Finnish epic *Kalevla* has more lines about the origin of beer and brewing than it does lines about the origin of mankind. Peko, the ancient Estonian and Finnish god of crops (particularly of barley and brewing), remains a national hero and is the subject of songs by current folk groups.

In Zulu mythology, Mbaba Mwana Waresa, the goddess of beer, rain, and the rainbow, is said to have made the first beer for humans to drink.

In Dogon mythology, Yasigi, the goddess of beer, dance, and masks, is depicted in statues holding a beer ladle while dancing.

In the Hindu pantheon, Soma, the Vedic moon god and reportedly the creator and father of all the other Vedic gods, lends his name to the sacred beverage Soma, drunk as a central part of Vedic rituals.

In Andean mythology, the Incas descended from the Sun. In thanksgiving, they worshiped the Sun during an annual fall festival at the end of the potato and maize harvest. At Machu Picchu, a citadel at the top of a mountainous jungle road along the Urubamba River in Peru, Corn Beer was central to the ceremony and was brewed by specially trained women brewers (priestesses). Large quantities of the beverage generally referred to as *Chichi* were shared with all the population. Similar festivals continue to this day in Peru, but with influences that date back to the conversion to Christianity in the seventeenth century.

Chicha (also called by many other local names) continues to be brewed throughout South America. Brewing is based on regional ways of life and replaces corn with yucca root, plantain, and a variety of fruits. Beer also continues to be a staple ingredient in traditional foods of El Salvador.

Tezcatzontecatl, associated with drunkenness and fertility, is the Aztec god of pulque, a fermented juice of the century plant (also known as agave americana or maguey). Pulque has qualities similar to those of beer.

# The Goddess Ninkasi

Ninkasi is the Sumer (southern Mesopotamian) goddess of *Sikaru*, the Sumerian word for beer. According to University of Oxford scholars, "The Hymn to Ninkasi," a prayer found on Sumerian clay tablets, was both a prayer and a way of remembering a recipe in a society that was not highly literate. The instructions called for combining a twice-baked bread known as bappir, which was a yeast source, with malted and soaked unmalted grains. Honey and dates were added to sweeten the brew. This mixture was put into a fermentation vessel for a specified time, filtered, and then transferred to a collecting vessel, from which it was drunk. Neither hops nor other bittering ingredients were added, making this brew considerably sweeter than modern beers.

According to the Sumerian myth, Ninkasi was born of "sparkling fresh water," a telling attribute for brewing beer, which she supposedly did every day. She is the prototype brewer, worshiped by men and women. Women brewed daily for their families, since the beverage did not keep beyond the day. Some women, chosen as priestesses of Ninkasi, served as brewers at the temple in her honor. As the goddess made to "satisfy the desire" and "sate the heart," Ninkasi remains revered.

**BREW WATCH**

In 1989, the San Francisco–based Anchor Brewing Company replicated the recipe as part of The Sumerian Beer Project. The limited-edition Anchor Steam Ninkasi Beer is described in Charlie Papazian's 1994 book, *Home Brewer's Companion* (New York: Avon Books).

Since 1992, the American Homebrewers Association has presented The Ninkasi Award to the brewer who gains the most points in the final round of the National Homebrew Competition, judged at the National Homebrewers Conference. Entrants gain points in 23 categories of Beer and the various categories of Mead and Cider. To win the title, a brewer must have at least two points (one bronze placement) from a beer entry.

# Recreating Early Brewing Methods

Early Egyptologists assumed that Egyptian beer was brewed as it was in Sumeria. Ideas changed with new research and an archeological discovery in the 1990s. Walls of Egyptian tombs illustrated a brewery and described the brewing process, which bears an uncanny similarity to the layout and activity in today's Sudanese breweries.

In 1996, Newcastle Breweries created a recipe based on Egyptian Exploration Society research on sediment from jars retrieved from a brewery in the Sun Temple of Nefertiti. About 1,000 bottles of Tutankhamon Ale were sold at Harrods in London; the proceeds went toward further research of brewing in ancient Egypt.

In 2002, the Yokohama-based Kirin Brewery Company connected with researchers at Waseda University in Japan to prove a different hypothesis about beer content and brewing methods. Kirin used the recipe found in the tomb of Niankhkhnum and Khnumuhotep of the Old Kingdom (2650–2180 B.C.E.) to prove that, even before the seventeenth century, when scientific understandings of yeast changed fermentation practices, Egyptians knew how to control microorganisms to ferment beer.

Kirin's reconstructed brew is reported to have an alcohol content of about 10 percent, well above the previously assumed 3 percent for everyday beer use. But images of feasts inscribed on the walls of the tombs supports the higher alcohol content and matches the myths about the blood-thirsty lioness goddess Sekhmet being tricked into getting drunk from consuming a large amount of red-colored beer, thus ending her slaughtering rampage and becoming docile.

Reports by people who tasted the beer recreated by Kirin Brewery say it contained very little carbonation, and therefore had no froth. Being lactic fermented, it had a higher lactic acid content than contemporary beers, but it nevertheless had a moderately bitter flavor and good body. Kirin brewers believe that because Egyptians did not use hops, their beer likely had a flavor balance resembling that of white wine.

# Reverence for the Craft

Beer is connected with the story of humanity from its earliest development of civilization. Expressions developed over the centuries refer to beer as a reason to gather together to have a good time, share good conversation, and be generous in sharing. And while beer is still considered the beverage of workers, the context in which beer grew as a part of the overall social order nevertheless places everyone on the same plane as goddesses and gods.

It is both awesome and awe inspiring that a glass of beer places you in the center of a past, present, and future that stays the same even as it changes. The current social milieu of pub crawling, pub games, and beer festivals is descended from a remote time and place. The Beer Institute website has this message:

> We hope you will find yourself at a party or other gathering where beer adds to your enjoyment. If so, we suggest you toast our primitive ancestors.

In so doing, we show our respect and reverence for the continuity of a craft and art that makes a beverage from the same ingredients and similar recipes found at the Cradle of Civilization. In drinking responsibly, we honor the passion and skill of the brewer and reverently accept this unique gift of the gods.

## The Least You Need to Know

- Almost every ancient culture viewed beer as a god-given drink that established a people's unique culture and religious practices and gave them a particular identity.

- Beer from Babylon in Mesopotamia was on the trade route to Egypt, probably used as barter for goods. From there, it spread throughout the world.

- Beer was a staple food item and a component of social activity.

- Beer became central to everyday and religious life in Egypt and is part of the on-going spirituality and religion of peoples worldwide.

- Because beer is an alcoholic beverage, we must use it respectfully and responsibly.

# Beer in the United States

## In This Chapter

- Bringing brews to the New World
- Observing the United States growing one brewery at a time
- Tracing the moves to uniformity of taste
- Comprehending the clash of social and religious agendas

The United States has cultural connections worldwide, yet our nation's early and primary influences came from the explorations by Spanish conquistadores, trading alliances with French voyageurs, and settlements by Dutch and British companies (followed by German and Bohemian immigrants). Each brought their distinctive beverage styles as a way of everyday life, with brewing of nutrition-laden Ales taking precedence over all other alcoholic beverages. By the middle of the nineteenth century, the Lager revolution had taken hold and held sway over Ales.

A century later, with the passage of Prohibition, beer fell into oblivion with all the other alcoholic beverages. Following repeal, a whole new business model emerged. This chapter brings you into the ever-changing role of beer and shares the dynamics of social, cultural, religious, and economic conditions in the "New World" through the past seven centuries.

# Beer in the New World

Tracing the story of beer in the New World has intrigued not only brewers, but also archaeologists, anthropologists, sociologists, historians, agronomists, and biologists. In 2007, archaeologist Glenna Dean conducted studies to show that Pueblo peoples in what is now the continental United States were brewing "a weak beer called 'tiswin,' made by fermenting kernels of corn."

Dean's academically based revelations counter claims that brewing did not exist on the continental United States prior to European intervention and corroborates Christopher Columbus's fifteenth-century report to Spain that "the Indians were in the habit of brewing." Beer historian Michael Jackson writes in his benchmark *The World Guide to Beer* (Prentice-Hall, 1975) that Columbus observed the natives of what we now call Central America "throw a handful of maize [corn] into an earthen jug, pour in a dollop of sap from the black birch tree, then fill the jug with water." Jackson concludes, "Natural fermentation did the rest."

And despite some claims to the contrary, it has been proven that the native populations in northern Mexico and the American Southwest were brewing a beer called Tesgüino, made by moistening corn until it sprouted. This mixture was ground, boiled, and allowed to ferment. The Apache were making Tesqüino into the nineteenth century, when the practice dwindled due to changes in their lifestyle with waves of settlers.

Perhaps the Spanish conquistadores didn't fully enjoy the beer prevalent throughout Central and South America in the sixteenth century. Alonso de Herrera built the first-known European-style brewery in the New World in Mexico in 1544, to produce beer closer to his taste and that of his fellow countrymen.

The same thing happened in the British Virginia colony along the Atlantic Coast. Sir Walter Raleigh reportedly brewed for his fellow settlers starting in 1587. However, they had little regard for his use of locally grown corn to make the malt and clamored for barley malt beer from England. Finally, in 1607, the first beer shipment from England arrived. On the other hand, the settlers in New Netherlands firmly established a local brewing culture starting in 1612, when Adrian Block and Hans Christiansen opened the first-known New World commercial brewery in New Amsterdam on Manhattan Island.

In 1632, the West India Company built a brewery on Brouwer's Straat (Brewers Street) in New Amsterdam under the direction of Governor Van Twiller. It was noted they used the wild hops found growing all around their premises. Somehow, when the British purchased New Amsterdam in 1664, these hops for the taking were ignored; instead, hops were imported from England at a high price.

Perhaps the most famous untold beer story is related to the Pilgrims. Textbooks explain that the Mayflower landed at Plymouth Rock, Massachusetts, instead of landing at its intended destination, near the Hudson River in the colony of Virginia, because food supplies were running low and the winter storms were forcing them off course. However, historians have failed to impart the full data, found in a passenger's diary: "Our victuals [are] much spent, especially our beere." It was of great concern to the sailors that they have enough beer for the return voyage to England. The Pilgrims were expected to make do when they landed. With a lot of help from the Wampanoag tribe, the Pilgrims survived and went on to prosper; the Wampanoag did not.

**BREW WATCH**

In 2007, the Mayflower Brewing Company was founded in Plymouth, Massachusetts, by Drew Brosseau, a tenth-generation grandson of John Alden, arguably the most essential person aboard the Mayflower. Young Alden was a beer barrel cooper, charged with making sure the supply of beer was safely kept during the ocean voyage. Men, women, and children drank it. Sailors had a ration of a gallon a day. The Mayflower Brewing Company now brews Pale Ale, Golden Ale, IPA, and Porter in the seventeenth-century style, and uses water from the wells the Pilgrims used.

# New World "Firsts"

Beer was everywhere in the New World. Almost every housewife brewed for the family, as part of sustaining a healthy lifestyle. At crossroads and settlements, small taverns came into being to provide shelter for travelers, and beer was expected to be available along with food. Eventually, when a settlement grew into a town, an enterprising family or sole brewer opened a brewery with an attached room where people could gather for socializing or purchase a pail of beer to take home.

The following catalog of "firsts" reveals that breweries emerged alongside the building of eighteenth-century towns and villages:

**1634:** Samuel Cole received the first license to operate a tavern in Boston.

**1637:** Captain Sedgwick was given control of the first brewery in Massachusetts Bay Colony.

**1639:** Sergeant Bauleton was placed in charge of a brewhouse in Providence, Rhode Island.

**1670:** Samuel Wentworth received a license to brew in Portsmouth, New Hampshire.

**1674:** Harvard opened a brewhouse. Students were served beer at each meal daily. It is reported, however, that divinity students burned down the five beer halls.

**1683:** The first brewery opened in Philadelphia. William Penn built a brewery on his estate in his colony (near present-day Bristol, Pennsylvania).

**1734:** Mary Lisle became the first "brewster" in the colonies, following the death of her father, who operated the Edinburgh Brewhouse in Philadelphia.

**BREW WATCH**

It is well known that eighteenth-century colonial American brewers used readily available ingredients, particularly flaked corn and molasses. Malted barley was imported from England at a high cost, and locally grown barley crops were not dependable, so colonial brewers used less malted barley and filled in with the more readily available locally grown corn. Imported hops were expensive, so they, too, were used sparingly. Benjamin Franklin, an outspoken advocate of economic independence for the colonies, spoke against dependence on foreign goods.

**1738:** The first brewery in what we call "the Deep South" opened in Georgia at Jekyll Island.

**BREW WATCH**

Homebrewer George Washington's handwritten recipe "To Make Small Beer" is in a notebook believed to be dated 1757. The original recipe is in the New York Public Library manuscript collections and is posted on the Internet. This is the beer he brewed at his Mount Vernon home.

**1765:** The British militia built the first brewery west of the Allegheny Mountains, at Fort Pitt (present-day Pittsburgh). The French built the first brewery outside the 13 colonies at their Kaskaskia settlement (in present-day Illinois).

**1786:** John Molson opened a brewery in Montreal. It is still operating.

**1789:** President George Washington issued his "Buy American" policy. He said he would drink only Porter made in America. His action was bolstered by Massachusetts, where the legislature passed a law to encourage brewers to make more beer and Ale, and for citizens to drink it in place of Imported Beer and Ale.

**BREW WATCH**

Ale in the eighteenth century was distinguished from "beer" by adding hops used as a preservative and a way to balance the sweetness of the malt with a bitter herbal flavor. The commonly available hops in the American colonies would have been English Kent Goldings.

**1812:** Thomas Jefferson began brewing beer. Originally, his wife, Martha, brewed beer for the household. After her death in 1782, brewing ceased.

**1812:** The first brewery opened in Hawaii.

**1815:** Joseph Coppinger published *The American Practical Brewer and Tanner.* An original copy is at the Hagley Museum and Library.

**1816:** Indiana gained designation as a state, and breweries opened in Richmond and New Harmony, each claiming to be the nineteenth state's first brewery.

**1819:** The first brewery opened in Rochester, New York.

**1819:** Thomas Holloway built the first steam engine to be used for beer production, for Frances Perot's Philadelphia brewery.

**1829:** David G. Yuengling opened his brewery in Pottsville, Pennsylvania. It continues as a family business.

**1830:** The first brewery opened in Buffalo, New York.

**1833:** The first brewery opened in Chicago.

**BREW WATCH**

Throughout the 1840s, a new wave of German immigrants to the United States included brewers making the newly developed Lagers. Beer is now defined as having two major categories: top-fermenting Ales and bottom-fermenting Lagers. Pffaulder Company in Rochester, New York, manufactured and sold bottom-fermenting vessels for Lager brewing worldwide throughout the nineteenth and twentieth century.

**1840:** John Wagner introduced Lager beer in Philadelphia.

**1844:** Fortmann and Company Brewery introduced Lager beer in Cincinnati.

**1847:** The first Lager brewery opened in Chicago.

**1848:** The first Lager brewery opened in Boston.

**BREW WATCH**

In 1844, Milwaukee got its start as "the brewing capital of the world" with the Best family. Frederick Pabst, a family member who had been a cabin boy on a Great Lakes steamer, renamed the company Pabst in 1889 and put a blue ribbon award symbol on the label, hence "Pabst Blue Ribbon." In 1848, August Krug opened Schlitz. Valentin Blatz opened his brewery in 1850. In 1855, Frederick Miller purchased the Plank Road Brewery and founded Miller Brewing Company, using yeast from Germany that he had carried in his pocket on the ocean voyage. Smart marketing moved Milwaukee beer nationwide and made these four companies industry leaders.

**1849:** The first California brewery opened in San Francisco.

**1855:** The first brewery opened in San Antonio, Texas.

**1856:** A commercial brewery opened near Latrobe, Pennsylvania, at the Monastery of the Benedictine Society of Saint Vincent's Abbey.

**1859:** Rocky Mountain Brewery opened as Colorado's first.

**1860:** Ferdinand Carre received a U.S. patent for the first commercial refrigeration machine.

**1862:** Idaho's first brewery opened in Lewiston.

**1863:** The Montana territory's first brewery opened in Virginia City.

**1865:** The first Arizona territory brewery opened in Tucson.

**1865:** Poughkeepsie brewer Matthew Vassar founded Vassar College as the first privately endowed U.S. school for women.

**1868:** John Siebel opened a brewing school in Chicago. It became the Siebel Institute of Technology.

*The American Brewer* magazine began publication.

**1875:** The first Lager beer was brewed in California.

**1876:** Louis Pasteur developed the process of stabilizing beer. He published a beer study showing how yeast organisms can be controlled.

**1886:** Alaska's first brewery opened in Juneau.

# The National Brewery Concept

The concept of a national brewery goes all the way back to December 16, 1810, when New York City brewer Joseph Coppinger wrote to President James Madison proposing a national brewery be built in Washington, D.C., to spur the growth of breweries in each state. Coppinger underscored the healthful benefits of beer, along with economic benefits of creating an American style that could be as much in demand as beers from Europe had been since settlers started coming to the New World. Madison favored Coppinger's idea but, at the time, was too occupied with domestic and international events that eventually culminated in the War of 1812.

By war's end, Coppinger had proposed his idea to Thomas Jefferson, who lent his support, but a national brewery failed to take hold. What did come to fruition in 1815 was publication of the highly prized guidebook *The American Practical Brewer and Tanner*. Jefferson utilized Coppinger's instructions in his newly established brewery at Monticello, and he further offered his brewery operation as a place others could come to learn the art, craft, and science of brewing during the optimum spring and fall brewing seasons. This story continues to be told at Monticello.

# The Beginnings of Macrobrewing

The storied Anheuser-Busch legacy started in 1852 with the founding of the Bavarian Brewery by George Schneider in St. Louis, Missouri. St. Louis at that time was burgeoning as "the gateway to America's frontier." In 1860, St. Louis soap maker Eberhard Anheuser acquired the Bavarian Brewery and renamed it E. Anheuser Company's Bavarian Brewery. In 1861, Anheuser's daughter Lilly married Adolphus Busch. Three years later, Busch joined the company.

According to company documents, the company brewed a variety of beers, including dark Bocks, light-colored Pilsners, hop Ale, and light Lagers. By 1872, Busch was on his way to making a wide mark, with plans for an enlarged brewing capacity and a bold logo showing an American eagle standing on a shield and jutting forth from an ornate double *A*. The message clearly indicated that Anheuser and America were commingled.

In 1876, the unity became a reality when Budweiser Lager Beer made its debut during the nationwide centennial celebration of the American Declaration of Independence of 1776. Over-riding the American preference for English Ales and German Lagers at that time, Busch chose to showcase his newly developed Pale Bohemian Lager and advertised it as "the United States' first national beer." Thus was born the connection with Budweiser and American patriotism that continues until the present. To be an American in the image of astute advertising from 1876 forward has been to drink a Pale Lager made with about 30 percent corn malt, as opposed to 100 percent barley or wheat malt, and to drink it to the exclusion of all other categories or styles of beer. One taste became fit for all.

Living in the whirl of change arising from the industrial and scientific revolutions of the nineteenth century, Adolphus Busch took full advantage of every innovation. He immediately adopted Louis Pasteur's 1876 discoveries surrounding yeast and made Anheuser-Busch the first American brewery to pasteurize beer. To further maintain freshness for a longer time and a greater distance, Busch developed iced "beer railroad cars" and refrigerator cars for long-distance shipping. In short order, the Budweiser brand blanketed the United States. Having reportedly "borrowed" the name Budweiser from the Bohemian town of Budweis, Busch then transposed the original Budweiser motto: "The Beer of Kings" became "The King of Beers."

But not even the empire Busch built could stem the onslaught of Prohibition.

# From Prohibition to After Repeal

Temperance always has been associated with the use of alcoholic beverages. With the privilege of enjoying a finely crafted beverage comes responsibility to do no harm to yourself or others. While self-chosen abstinence has been associated with religious beliefs, prohibition through legislation that makes alcohol use illegal arises from individuals and groups seeking to impose upon everyone a particular standard of behavior.

The impetus arose from a moral or social implication that, because some people abuse the privilege, everyone must cease and desist. The gravest abuses of alcohol use of any kind arose with abuses of the Industrial Revolution, poverty stemming from migration from rural to urban environments, and displacement of groups of people from traditional community-centric life to a life of fending for oneself. When people facing a harsh existence could find escape only in getting drunk, people suffered. However, instead of addressing the conditions causing people to abuse alcohol, moralists attacked and admonished the workers, not the industrialists.

The American Society for the Promotion of Temperance was formed in Boston in 1826. By 1829, its membership had grown to 100,000 members. U.S. Prohibition laws began in Maine in 1846 and spread throughout the nation. The Women's Temperance Union was founded in 1874. Its members established a Department of Scientific Temperance in schools and colleges nationwide and promoted free public drinking fountains as a way to get people to drink water instead of beer to quench their thirst. More than 20 temperance organizations emerged nationwide, few of which actually addressed the real underlying causes for abuse.

In the wake of the worldwide economic crisis of the 1870s and 1880s, the brewing industry itself was undergoing change as mergers and takeovers by syndicates began in the United States and spread worldwide. Small breweries had already begun to falter and fail. With the founding of the Anti-Saloon League in 1893, Prohibition gained its final impetus.

On January 16, 1919, the 18th Amendment to the U.S. Constitution was ratified, making the manufacture, sale, and transportation of alcohol illegal. It was scheduled to take effect a year later, on January 16, 1920. House of Representatives Bill No. 6810 presented in May by Representative Volstead established the apparatus for the enforcement of Prohibition. Volstead's bill was passed on October 10 and vetoed by President Wilson on October 27, but a Congressional vote overrode Wilson's veto.

Simultaneous with Prohibition came ways to flaunt the law. Three lasting effects that continue to haunt are the income tax to make up for the loss from taxes on alcoholic beverages; the manufacture of sweet drinks, now considered a major cause of obesity; and the loss of a vibrant brewing industry encompassing breweries of all sizes crafting a wide variety of styles. Instead of lessening social ills and decreasing the cost of government, the opposite happened. Even some of the staunchest supporters of Prohibition, including John D. Rockefeller, pronounced "The Great Experiment" a failure.

In 1931, the American Legion voted for a referendum of national Prohibition. The pendulum was now swinging in the opposite direction. Montana repealed its state Prohibition laws in 1926. Other states quickly followed.

The Cullen–Harrison Act, signed by President Franklin D. Roosevelt on March 22, 1933, instituted a tax of $5 per barrel on beer and allowed states that did not have state Prohibition laws to sell 3.2 percent *ABW* or 4.0 percent *ABV* beer and wine. Then on December 5, 1933, the 21st Amendment was fully ratified—federal laws enforcing Prohibition were repealed.

**BREW WATCH**

Readily available "near beers" that were brewed during Prohibition included Pablo by Pabst, Famo by Schlitz, Vivo by Miller, Lux-O by Stroh, and Bevo by Anheuser-Busch.

**DEFINITIONS**

**ABW (alcohol by weight)** is an alternate measure indicating the alcohol level in beer. Convert ABW to ABV by multiplying the ABW percent by 1.25.

**ABV (alcohol by volume)** is the standard in the United States indicating the alcohol level in beer, measured by percent. The higher the percent number, the higher the alcohol.

**Adjuncts** are ingredients other than malted barley or malted wheat to make the mash.

During 1934, 756 breweries were back in operation. Although the industry never recovered its original vibrancy, innovations were on the upswing, particularly the move from bottles to cans. On January 24, 1935, the first canned beer was sold in the test market of Richmond, Virginia, as a venture between the American Can Company and Krueger Brewing Company of Newark, New Jersey. Soon afterward, Schlitz introduced the cone-top can, made by Continental Can Company.

By 1935, breweries that had found ways to diversify and remain in business during Prohibition began to buy up smaller breweries that had less capital to compete in a changing economy. The larger companies either closed down the smaller ones or absorbed their products. Ingredients and styles shifted away from the classic European Ales and Lagers to recipes that satisfied a new taste that had to replace the sugar-laden drinks made during Prohibition. The shift, thus, was toward a "sweeter, lighter" beer, achieved through the use of flaked corn, corn syrup, and other sweeteners.

With the shortages during World War II came the use of *adjuncts* to replace wheat and barley malt. With a large part of the male population serving in the military, marketing began to entice women to drink a lighter beer. New generations with no historic references were more swayed by advertising than by quality and diversity of products. They chose brand over style, peer pressure over content, and temperature over taste. But change was again on the horizon.

**BREW WATCH**

In 1959 and 1960, Coors, of Golden, Colorado, introduced the aluminum can and the aluminum can top. Pittsburgh Brewing Company introduced the tab-top can in 1962 and the "ring pull" can in 1965. In 1969, canned beer outsold bottled beer, and brewers selling nationwide were tailoring the size of cans to local and regional preferences.

# The Rise of the Homebrewer

The story of homebrewing after Prohibition's repeal is a cautionary tale, with the moral being "Don't party until you proofread." A clerk omitted the words "and homebrewing" when copying the original Congressional Bill into its final form to be signed by President Roosevelt in 1933. No one noticed the words were missing. The document read only "home winemaking" as legal. Not until 1978 and President Jimmy Carter's signature did homebrewing become legal in February 1979. Thus began the slow but steady change to the beer industry, with the consumer as homebrewer taking the lead in bringing back many styles that ceased to be brewed after Anheuser-Busch heralded Budweiser, a uniform Lager, as "the American beer" in 1876.

However, because the 21st Amendment largely leaves regulation of alcohol to the states, not all states legalized homebrewing in 1979. As of 2012, homebrewing is not legal in Alabama and Mississippi.

**BREW WATCH**

The three-tier system set up by the 21st Amendment to the U.S. Constitution requires the production brewery to sell its product to a distributor, who, in turn, sells the product to a store, restaurant, bar, or tavern, where it is sold to a consumer who is of legal age. Brewpubs may sell directly to a consumer of legal age under certain conditions determined by state and federal licenses. Everyone has to apply for and receive a license to sell any kind of alcoholic beverage.

The American Homebrewers Association (AHA), founded in 1978 by author and Brewers Association president Charlie Papazian, organizes competitions and provides information about beer in general and homebrewing in particular. While there are 30,000 members of the AHA, it is estimated that "nearly one million Americans brew beer and make wine at home at least once a year."

With the legalization of homebrewing in 1979, homebrewers began pushing the envelope for Craft brewers to bring back "lost" brews, particularly Ales with multiple layers of flavors. How those got lost is part of the commercial brewing story.

**BREW WATCH**

Large breweries sought to define American taste with a single product that did not require much thought. By nature, Lagers are less complex than Ales. However commercial brewers use ingredients such as rice and corn to "lighten" the taste of two-row barley or wheat. Thus, it is a bland beer when compared with the more robust styles from Craft breweries.

## The Least You Need to Know

- Early settlers to the New World and Colonial America followed by immigrants to the young United States significantly influenced the American beer culture.

- The brewing industry grew with the settlement of the continental United States, east coast to west.

- The number of breweries in the United States (and worldwide) began to decline during the 1900s as larger operations bought out (and sometimes closed down) smaller breweries. This accelerated with Prohibition and its aftermath.

- After homebrewing again was legalized in 1979 the movement began for return to Classic styles of Ales and Lagers with diverse flavor profiles.

# The Craft Beer Comeback

## In This Chapter

- Meeting the "culture of Craft"
- Taking brewing back to its beginnings
- Learning what discerning consumers of beer want
- Looking at the modern-era beer industry
- Developing a Craft brand and band of loyalists

In this chapter, we connect your adventurous, inquisitive spirit as a part of the Craft beer saga of quality beer and food in the context of a responsible, uplifting lifestyle. Then we meet the brewers who have been taking beer back to its original traditions—made local and served fresh, to be savored and not swilled. Finally, we traverse regions across the United States where Craft beer has been gaining a special place in the culture of communities.

# What's the Craft?

"Craft beer," as a twentieth-century designation, came with the re-emergence of beer brewed in small quantities and sold both on draft and in bottles and cans close to the brewery, as well as offered on draft at the brewery. There's no hiding the ingredients or the process—no secrets among homebrewers. The conversation runs something like this: "You're a brewer? Hey, here's the recipe. Try it. Let me know how it turns out. Bring a sample, and let's drink it and talk about it. Let me know what you changed and what you tweaked, discovered, and uncovered in your process."

An email notice of the tapping of a new brew at a brewpub typically includes listing ingredients along with the description. Here's an example from Bloomington Brewing Company (Indiana). Head brewer Floyd Rosenbaum learned to brew in Alaska in the 1970s. He says, "I met Alaskans who were brewing with ingredients other than hops, and I developed a taste for diverse ingredients." Floyd homebrewed for about 20 years before stepping in as a professional brewer. "I don't use *fining agents*," he explains. "I love the traditional cask and wooden barrel to ripen."

 **DEFINITIONS**

**Fining agents** are added at the end of the boil step or in the fermenter to clear the beer of haze that can come from suspended yeast, proteins from the malt, and polyphenols from hops and malt.

And so it goes coast to coast with people who are interested in Craft beer. So when asked what's special about Craft beer, it's simply a way of life that's a cut above the ordinary. It's about engaging the life of the mind and finding zest in all possibilities. What you hear is the voice of ordinary people over the drumbeat of mass advertising. People are in charge and driving the industry.

In business terms, it's a market-driven demand, not a marketing-driven enticement. The baseball stadium is the bellwether. While "the big boys" can demand the contracts for exclusivity, team owners are standing up. Kansas City is a sterling case in point, with local Boulevard Brewing in full sight. This example of standing up for the fans has had ripple effects across the United States. Fans supporting local teams want local brews. How about that for brawn and brains?

# Taking Beer Back to Its Beginnings

Fritz Maytag's purchase of Anchor Brewing Company (San Francisco, California) in 1965 is viewed as a benchmark for the concept of keeping beer local, fresh, innovative, and fully flavorful. Maytag is credited with saving the quintessential American-produced steam beer and creating recipes for six other distinctively flavored beers. Anchor Steam used only barley malt and whole hops for Ales and Lagers that stand with the best of traditional European brews. News of Maytag's bravado traveled across the United States just about the time post–World War II Europe was beckoning travelers across the pond, exposing us to the divergent tastes of England, Scotland, Ireland, Germany, Belgium, and Holland.

In October 1976, the boldest act of all was the opening of the New Albion Brewing Company in Sonoma, California, by homebrewer Jack McAuliffe, along with business partners Suzy Denison and Jane Zimmerman. At the time, McAuliffe spoke of the influence of Fritz Maytag and the beers of Scotland, which he drank while stationed abroad with the U.S. Navy. He further credited University of California–Davis professor Michael Lewis with helping to grow the Craft industry through an intern partnership with New Albion.

During a telephone conversation to share his story, McAuliffe described the summers when University of California–Davis students came as apprentices to his brewery to learn hands-on operation: "Even though it was a small brewery, we had to do all the things a midsize or large brewery does"—including meeting payroll, paying bills, ordering supplies, brewing, bottling, shipping, working with distributors, maintaining the plant, and being an active participant in the brewing industry and the community-at-large. "They became immersed in the full scope of operating a brewery."

Acknowledged as the first twentieth-century microbrewery, New Albion continues to have influence, despite having operated for only five years. Every subsequent brewery that opened in the 1980s credited Jack McAuliffe as its inspiration and guide, and many among us cite both Anchor Steam and New Albion beer as our first taste of how real beer could and should taste.

Looking back, McAuliffe comments, "I was just out there trying to build a brewery. The industry was at its lowest point in 1976, with only 19 or so breweries. Today there are 2,000, with over 1,000 new breweries being planned. I'm truly amazed at the growth. More than 100,000 people are employed in the United Stated brewing industry. That's the part that amazes me. It was never in my imagination."

**BREW WATCH**

As a tribute to Jack McAuliffe, in 2010, Sierra Nevada Brewing Company released Jack and Ken's Ale, brewed collaboratively by McAuliffe and Ken Grossman, to mark Sierra Nevada's 30th anniversary. A companion video highlights the pioneers who "transformed American into the most exciting brewing nation in the world." Starting in January 2013, Jack McAuliffe's "New Albion Ale" is again available, with its release under the New Albion label, brewed by the Boston Beer Company, as a tribute to the significance of the New Albion Brewing Company and the enduring legacy of Craft brewer Jack McAuliffe.

A specific point McAuliffe feels needs to be corrected is the idea that Craft brewers feel combative against the big brewers. "It has nothing to do with David and Goliath," he says "I've talked with Fritz Maytag; I've talked with other brewers. I don't get it, they don't get it—why the headlines about David and Goliath? We're not enemies. We each make beer our own way and hope people like it."

During a visit to Schlafly Brewing Company in St. Louis, Schlafly staff voiced this same point about being professionals in an industry that has room for a lot of choices. After the July 2008 purchase of Anheuser-Busch (A-B) by InBev, a Belgian-based company, I was expecting some gloating—or at least a dig or two about A-B suffering the same plight it had inflicted on regional brewers over the years. However, instead of alluding to the animal kingdom food chain analogy, people at Schlafly spoke of the contributions Anheuser-Busch had made to the greater St. Louis community during its years as a locally based enterprise.

# What Craft Brewers and Discerning Consumers Want

In 2007, I was invited to a special food–beer dinner at the Ruth's Chris Steak House in Indianapolis. A dedicated Craft beer columnist, I was hesitant about attending until I learned that George F. Reisch would be presiding over the event.

Reisch is a fifth-generation brewmaster whose forbearers have a colorful connection with the U.S. brewing story that begins around 1826 in the grand duchy of Baden, close to the Rhine River. A U.S. envoy stopped in the small village of Niederhausen and invited men to come to the United States to start breweries and wineries. Seventeen-year-old Frank Sales Reisch resolved to become a brewer and *cooper* and immigrate to the United States.

In 1832, after three years as an apprentice and another three years as a journeyman in Alsace, Frank traveled by ship to New Orleans and, according to family history, "worked his way across the states of Kentucky, Ohio, Indiana, and Illinois, earning a living as a cooper and looking for a place to build his brewery." The story continues:

> As soon as he could save enough money he bought a quarter section (forty acres) of white oak timberland. During the day he cleared the land and tilled the soil, building a house, workshop, stable, cribs, and a granary. At night he made barrels by candlelight. In 1847 he bought an acre of land in Springfield, Illinois, and began construction of the large underground cellars where the beer would be fermented and stored. He did all the work himself. He dug a well, made the aging vats, and built a 3-story frame building 20 feet by 24 feet above the cellars. His first brew kettle was copper and had an 8-barrel capacity. In the winter he brewed enough beer to meet the summer demand. He also cut ice from nearby ponds and rivers to keep the beer cool in the summer. The first Reisch Beer was sold in 1849.

**DEFINITIONS**

A **cooper** is someone who makes and repairs casks such as barrels and tubs. In early brewing, making wooden mash tuns was part of the work of coopers. Because wooden barrels are used to age beers, coopers sometimes are assigned the task of fining, or aging, beers. An added responsibility might also be to clean wooden vessels at a brewery. Another term in England is an abroad cooper, the person who is responsible for tasting the barrel upon delivery to a tavern to make sure its quality was maintained during transport.

Reisch Gold Top was available in the mid-1950s. Having soldiered on through Prohibition and the Great Depression, Reisch was an example of the American spirit. By 1966, Reisch Brewing was struggling to keep a creditable market share. When an offer came to buy the brewery, the great-grandsons of Frank Sales Reisch sold, and young George moved with his family to Wisconsin. Describing himself as an avid homebrewer, having learned from his father, George attended the University of Wisconsin and earned a degree in chemistry while working at the Joseph Schlitz Brewing Co. During the summers, he worked as a research assistant at Miller Brewing Co.

"Anheuser-Busch hired me right out of school," recalls George. That was in 1979. Twenty-eight years later, his own son is preparing to continue as a sixth-generation brewer. Says George, "When you're born into a German brewing family, a lot of traditions surround you, especially the visuals and aromas that are part of life."

For George, through family tradition, "beer is the servant of food." Over the years, he developed recipes for both. "Beer is a beverage of moderation that is very social. Beer is woven through thousands of years of our social fabric connected with food. It was able to be served at every meal to every member of the family—small beers for the youngest."

Reisch spoke of different beers as having different personalities. And he spoke of consumer choice, something he feels Prohibition took away. As a college student, George was part of the generation moving toward choice.

In the 1970s and 1980s, Anheuser-Busch was hiring a team of 100 college graduates to promote A-B beers on college campuses. That was when people like me came to feel that A-B was marginalizing campus life. Their emphasis on peer pressure, crowd culture, one-taste, and excess through binging events at fraternities were at odds with the desire for independent thinking and choice, moderation, and a quality lifestyle.

What Craft brewers and discerning consumers truly wanted in the 1960s, 1970s, and 1980s was close-to-home small breweries with a distinctive brand (such as New Albion) and the ability to brew at home—legally. The "illegal" designation had been a travesty since 1933, and it took 45 years for congressional oversight to be rectified.

In Los Angeles, in 1974, homebrewer Merlin Elhardt and home winemaking shop owner John Daume joined forces to launch a club named the Maltose Falcons, believed to be the first modern U.S. homebrew club. Like many other home winemaking supply store owners, Elhardt had been selling brewing supplies since the repeal of Prohibition. By 1978, members of the club were active in legalizing homebrewing in California. Having helped to accomplish that, the club worked with California Sen. Alan Cranston to submit a U.S. Senate bill to legalize homebrewing throughout the United States. And therein lies what I've come to consider a convergence of seemingly unrelated events to mark 1978 as a turning point from one-taste-fits-all to a full spectrum of tastes and the cutting-edge impetus for the modern professional Craft industry in the United States.

Along with the significance of homebrew clubs such as the Maltose Falcons, whose members included Paul Camusi and Ken Grossman (who made history in 1980 with the opening of Sierra Nevada Brewing Company in Chico, California), was the founding of the American Homebrewers Association and publication of the first issue of the newsletter *Zymergy* in 1978 in Boulder, Colorado, by Charlie Matzen and Charlie Papazian. Even though *The Complete Joy of HomeBrewing* was not published until 1980, author Charlie Papazian had been perfecting his now-famous technique since 1970, when he began beermaking. His mantra of "Relax. Don't worry. Have a homebrew." injected the humor and lightness that still carries even the most timid among us into fully appreciating the passion, science, art, and Craft that goes into brewing the beers we savor.

And therein lies the story of two dedicated, enterprising individuals in Seattle, Washington, who turned their attention to educating the larger population of consumers to appreciate great taste and connect with their local brewing histories. In Seattle, brewing began in 1854, when it was a newly established logging town. Antonio B. Rabbeson founded the Washington Brewery. For Charles and Rose Ann Finkel, the mission for tasteful alcohol consumption started in the 1960s with educating consumers about wine. Deciding that beer deserved equal attention, the Finkels traveled throughout the United Kingdom, Germany, and Belgium to find beers to import to the United States. In sync with homebrewers' desire to bring back the old classics that had gone "out of fashion," Charles Finkel reportedly worked with brewers at Samuel Smith's, Yorkshire's oldest brewery (founded in Tadcaster in 1758), to revive Oatmeal Stout. The dark, dry Stout, with a new label designed by Finkel, was a success, as was the Porter. Thus validated, Merchant du Vin was founded in 1978 and continues to be recognized as "America's Premier Specialty Beer Importer," setting the standard for other companies that began to appear throughout the United States.

But one other 1978 event earns our attention, as it did that of Charles and Rose Ann Finkel, who came upon the newly published *The World Guide to Beer* edited, by Michael Jackson, already renowned world-wide for his expertise in wine. *The World Guide to Beer* is the lodestar for understanding and appreciating the nuances of beers according to cultural, geographic, and national standards. Jackson not only discusses ingredients, brewing methods, the artistry of labels, and the uniqueness of glassware, but also places a style within the context of change over time. With Jackson, we get into Craft beer as a way of life that places quality at the center.

# Entrepreneurial Women in Craft Brewing

Not by their own volition have women been supplanted as the brewers of choice. With the emergence of Abbey Beers and the advent of the Industrial Revolution, women lost their place of prestige. Nevertheless, the following is a list of women and their breweries that broke through barriers and serve up wonderful Craft brews.

**www.stoudts.com**   In the 1980s United States, it was rare to find women working as professional brewers, much less as founders and owners of breweries. When Carol and Ed Stoudt opened Stoudt's Brewing Company in 1987 in Adamstown, Pennsylvania, the event was hailed as a "first." No one believed Carol was brewing, having learned the traditional way by apprenticing under brewer Karl Strauss. Now the brewery is part of a tourist destination complex in Lancaster County as a companion to artisan bread, food, and antiques.

**http://intercoursebrewingco.com**   In 2008, Nicole Courides, a recent college graduate with no traditional job prospects, opened Intercourse Brewing Company, named after the Lancaster County, Pennsylvania, town. Within two years, Courides proved her Ales were consumer worthy by gaining multistate accounts within the region.

**www.lostcoast.com**   In 1990, Barbara Groom and Wendy Pound opened Lost Coast Brewery in Humboldt County's Old Town Eureka in California.

**www.sixriversbrewery.com**   Meredith Maier and Talia Nachshon increased the Humboldt County "female brewery owner" demographics in 2006 with Six Rivers Brewery.

**www.newbelgium.com**   New Belgium Brewing Company, in Fort Collins, Colorado, expanded out of its basement homebrewing setup in 1991. Jeff Lebesch brewed, and Kim Jordan served as bottler, sales rep, distributor, marketer, and financial planner—all of which made her president of the third-largest U.S. microbrewery.

**www.newglarusbrewing.com**   The New Glarus Brewing Company was founded in New Glarus, Wisconsin, in 1993 by Deborah Carey, who raised the capital and became its president. Carey is cited as "the first woman in the United States to found and operate a brewery." Her husband, Dan Carey, a Diploma Master Brewer from the University of California–Davis, gained experience brewing in Germany and built his first brewery in Helena, Montana. He followed it with 47 others, including New Glarus.

**www.blackstonebrewery.com** Kent Taylor and Stephanie Weins opened Blackstone Restaurant and Brewery in Nashville, Tennessee, in 1994. They created a relationship with Schlafly Brewing in St. Louis when Dave Miller, the Schlafly Tap Room head brewer, became head brewer at Blackstone. In 2011, with Schlafly looking to expand into Tennessee, the breweries formed an agreement for Schlafly to brew in Blackstone's newly expanded production facility. Although different from the concept of *contract brewing*, such "brewing independently yet cooperatively" alliances are becoming part of the Craft brewing scene as production breweries and brewpubs seek to expand without building new physical plants.

**DEFINITIONS**

According to the Brewers Association, a **contract brewing** company is "a business that hires another brewery to produce its beer. It can also be a brewery that hires another brewery to produce additional beer."

**www.jackalopebrew.com** Bailey Spaulding and Robyn Virball opened Jackalope Brewing Company in East Nashville; beer writers erroneously touted it as Tennessee's first female-run brewery (with no references to Blackstone with a shared female/male ownership). What further makes Jackalope unique is its reliance on preopening social media. This phenomenon has been noted across the United States, with owners of other recently opened breweries and brewpubs working hard to gain a dedicated following before tapping and pouring the first brew.

**www.portneufvalleybrewing.com** Homebrewer Penny Pink opened Portneuf Valley Brewing in Pocatello, Idaho, in 1996 inside Dudley's Sports Bar and Grill. In 2002, Owner and Brew Mistress Penny Pink began production in the refurbished East Idaho Brewing company building, which was further renovated to open a brewpub in 2006.

This impressive list of entrepreneurial women in brewing owes something to two somewhat unsung heroes in the modern brewing industry. When Jack McAuliffe opened the New Albion Brewery in October 1976, two other partners were listed: Suzy Denison and Jane Zimmerman. There's no further reference to them as Craft brewery investors, but for the record, we salute Mesdames Denison and Zimmerman for their foresight and gutsiness in breaking new ground.

It has been a struggle for women to gain positions in commercial, professional brewing if they did not found their own companies. Teri Fahrendorf, a Siebel Institute graduate, is credited as among the first to overcome the prejudice against women brewing in production breweries and brewpubs. She persevered and earned the title of Brewmaster. During her 19-year career (1988–2007), she won eight medals in Great American Beer Competitions before retiring to found the Pink Boots Society, which "was created to empower women beer professionals to advance their careers in the Beer Industry through Education." Check it out at http://pinkbootssociety.org.

**BREW WATCH**

The 2012 documentary *For the Love of Beer,* produced and directed by Alison Grayson (www.amazon.com/The-Love-of-Beer/dp/B009MMC4LK), features Teri Fahrehdorf; Sarah Pederson, journalist, radio host, and author of *Craft Beers of the Pacific Northwest: A Beer Lover's Guide to Oregon, Washington, and British Columbia (Timber Press, 2011)*; Lisa Morrison, publican of Saraveza Bottle Shop and Pasty Tavern in Portland, Oregon; and Brewmaster Tonya Cornett.

# Why Is Craft Beer Central to Our Lives?

People in the Craft beer industry at all levels are observing a consumer movement to prefer quality artisan products, particularly locally made. The concept of a sustainable culture in all aspects of our lives has grown beyond the rubric of reduce, reuse, reclaim, and repurpose. We now look as well at how we sustain ourselves and our local and regional enterprises.

According to Jim Schembre, National General Manager of World Class Beer, "The American consumer is now circling around and embracing several new concepts that include great food, successful entrepreneurs, and anything that reflects local." Jim is a third-generation member of a family owned beer distribution company. In the 1990s, he opted to represent small Craft breweries from across the United States to increase their market presence in the state of Indiana. In so doing, he educated a largely macrobrew consumer base about the delights of flavorful brews. In turn, this growing consumer base for quality Ales and Lagers inspired the growth of Artisan brewing in Indiana.

Charlie Papazian, author of *The Complete Joy of Homebrewing, Third Edition* (HarperResource, 2003) and founder of The Brewer's Association, underscores how "Choice, diversity, information, education, grassroots activism, quality, personality, passion, flavor (both in the real and metamorphic sense) serve as the foundation of the growing commitment to a life of quality. Craft brewers and Craft beer enthusiasts have been and continue to be pioneers in developing a world that contributes to the pleasure of our everyday life."

Similarly, Bob Mack, web designer at World Class Beer, describes Craft beer consumers as "stepping up" to a quality lifestyle that includes responsible management of time, nourishment (food and beverages), and exercise. To serve a growing population of discerning consumers, Mack designed an educational program for World Class Beer sales personnel, who in turn educate the point of sales personnel in retail shops. But what really happens is that the consumer coming to the store or tavern or restaurant learns more than what beer goes best with the planned menu or the special event. Craft beer is both personality-laden because of the brewing team and place-enhanced because of the location of the brewery. Every glass, bottle, or can of beer has a story to share.

Julia Herz, Brewer's Association Craft Beer program director, regards Craft beer as a "living history." She agrees that each glass displays the creativity and passion of its maker and the complexity of its ingredients. Herz equally alludes to every Craft beer consumer possessing a story of that "aha" moment when Craft beer became central to their lives as a way of seeing things more clearly, understanding something more fully, appreciating someone more deeply.

# The Modern-Era Beer Industry

Here's a quick look at how the modern-era beer industry reflects multiple levels of brewing for private and public use:

- Brewpubs emerged as a combination of food and beer prepared and served on the premises. "Pub food" is usually simple and predictable, based on the location. Most brewpubs will fill *growlers* for takeout. Some brewpubs also bottle or can and fill kegs for sale off-premises.

- Gastropubs brew beer to be sold on the premises, but the concept of food is referred to as *cuisine*, usually reflecting a particular culture, such as a Belgian gastropub.

- Breweries with a beer garden make their beer mainly to be sold off-premises, but they also sell pints on the premises, to be enjoyed in a space outside the brewery. Food service is either catered or brought in.

- Breweries with a full-service restaurant are larger than brewpubs. They have a more extensive menu and the dining area might be separated from the brewery itself.

- Production breweries brew beer to be sold off-premises. Some production breweries have a tasting room and also offer tours. No food is served.

- Commercial breweries are sometimes referred to as macrobrewries because of the volume of beer brewed on a daily, monthly, and yearly basis. They do not fit the Brewers Association guidelines as a Craft brewery.

**DEFINITIONS**

A **growler** is a late-nineteenth-century/early-twentieth-century container (usually a tin bucket or pail) used to carry beer from a tavern to the home. In the United States, it came back into use after the repeal of Prohibition. Although there are many fanciful explanations for the name *growler,* it is generally accepted that the name comes from the growling sound of carbon dioxide bubbles escaping from the vents on the cover as the pail was jostled during carrying. Most Artisan breweries and brewpubs now offer carryout in glass bottles that are still called growlers; some offer a smaller size in plastic, dubbed howlers.

Brewing companies are designated as national, regional, and specialty Craft brewers. National brewers brew beer on a mass scale and sell in all (or almost all) states. This group includes Anheuser-Busch-InBev, SAB-Miller, and Molson Coors Brewing Company. Regional brewers serve a multistate area and include Pittsburgh Brewing Company, Yuengling, Latrobe Brewing Company, and High Falls Brewing Company. Specialty Craft brewers include brewpubs and microbreweries serving a single neighborhood, metropolitan area, or state, or can serve a region or selected states.

The Brewers Association, the not-for-profit trade group that tabulates production statistics for U.S. breweries, notes that, based on 2011 beer sales volume, of the top 50 overall brewing companies, 36 are small and independent Craft-brewing companies. Furthermore, during the last 15 years, Craft brewing has increased from 1 percent of the overall beer market to nearly 6 percent.

In the space we have, we can't touch on the totality of the swirl of activity that makes up the brewing industry. We hope we've gotten you curious enough that you'll want to investigate on your own by visiting breweries and asking questions about the craft.

# The Phenomenal Growth of the Craft Beer Industry

According to Brewers Association statistics, demand for Craft beer is greater than the supply, even though most of us live within 10 miles of a microbrewery, brewpub, or beer bar specializing in Craft brews. Some communities have become magnets for Craft brewing—where, within walking distance, you can find two to five establishments, each with a distinctive brand. In early settlements throughout the United States, local taste dictated the kind of beer brewed. A brewer who wanted to stay in business had to satisfy customers first and experiment with new tastes second. The same holds true today.

Most Craft breweries are local and regional; only a handful sell nationwide, appealing to a wide demographics. Early on, the macrobreweries carve out a niche for one reasonably lucrative company brew to fit all tastes so that they can generate income for investors. Yet even their management teams recognize the discerning tastes of consumers and have been buying up successful small Craft breweries to gain market share. For the biggest breweries, it's a matter of gains and profits. And while the microbreweries need to be attentive to growth in order to stay in business, their need to satisfy investors or stockholders is less pressing. Taking risks is more prevalent because producing a good beer is essential in gaining and keeping a following.

Nevertheless, ambiance, atmosphere, and attitude play equal parts in developing a brand and a band of loyalists. Labeling and packaging influence a nondiscriminating customer buying a take-along for a cookout. Placement on shelves in a supermarket or proximity to the window in a bottle shop impacts sales. Word-of-mouth carries weight. While advertising isn't a major budget item for microbreweries, marketing and merchandising are critical issues. Wearing a brewery's T-shirt or hat is on par with following sports teams.

Charismatic owners and brewers, and glitzy locations and events featured on the Beer Channel (www.thebeerchannel.net) or the Travel Channel (www.travelchannel.com/topics/beer/index.html) draw attention to their products and locations. Sam Calgione, founder of Dogfish Head Brewery in Delaware, garners attention with Brew Masters on the Discovery Channel (http://dsc.discovery.com/tv/brew-masters). Upland Brewing Company labels appear regularly on NBC's long-running series *Parks and Recreation*.

**BREW WATCH**

Buffalo Bill Owens opened Buffalo Bill's Micro-Brewery in Hayward, California, and caught attention nationwide. Owens's six-barrel brewhouse subsequently became a model for other microbreweries. While some argue that Buffalo Bill's was the first brewpub in the United States, Grant's Brewery Pub, founded in Yakima in 1982, generally is considered to be the first microbrewery in the Northwest.

A number of brewpubs and breweries have gained national attention, but most are known only locally and regionally. Unless you're from the Northwest, you might not know that picturesque brewpubs proliferate throughout the greater Portland area. Brothers Mike and Bert McMenamin have rescued, renovated, restored, and revamped close to 100 historic buildings, with amenities beyond excellent brews. The listing online at www.mcmenamins.com/pubs inspires awe.

The sprawling Oldenberg Brewery and Entertainment Complex in Fort Mitchell, Kentucky, requires a whole day or more to explore.

Frankenmuth Brewery, established in 1862 in Michigan's professed "Little Bavaria," on the Cass River, is another destination place. The picturesque town of Frankenmuth sits between Flint and Detroit.

Three Floyds, in Munster, Indiana, Dark Lord Day is a magnet for hopheads worldwide to converge at the brewery annually on the last Saturday in April.

Crown Brewing in Crown Point, Indiana, might beckon as one of the notorious locations. The brewery is on the site of the jailhouse from which John Dillinger escaped in 1934. The 2009 film *Public Enemy*, starring Johnny Depp, has footage of the brewery that opened a year earlier.

So wherever you go, don't just drink a brew—ask about the story of the building and the neighborhood, ask to meet the brewers and learn their stories, and find out what makes their brews unique, distinctive, inspiring. And share something about how and why you got into the Craft beer scene. After all, you make it happen. Without you, there would be no comeback or growth. Cheers!

## The Least You Need to Know

- The return of Craft beer grew from a post–World War II grass-roots movement of people wanting to regain choice in the world's oldest beverage.

- Microbreweries grew from the ranks of homebrewers and college-trained brewers, along with the traditional guild system of learning and earning experience.

- Craft brewing invites a growing number of models from the neighborhood brewpub to the regional or national micro-production brewery.

- Consumers are part of the cutting-edge scene, gaining knowledge and demanding excellence.

# Understanding Beer

From the beginning, all beer was handcrafted. Beer was beer, first as top fermented Ales and then also as bottom-fermented Lagers. Each brew became special through that individual brewer's art, craft, taste, and science.

Craft beer designation came about in the twentieth century to differentiate the micro- and nanobrewers from the macrobrewers—that is, to recognize the small and very small batches made by a person as being distinct from the large and very large batches made by machines overseen by a person. Naturally, hands-on brewing and technology-assisted brewing require different levels of participation. In Part 2, we explore the many facets of beer brewed in different settings.

# So Exactly What Is Beer?

## In This Chapter

- Considering the many facets of beer
- Utilizing preferred water and malt
- Finding and adding quality hops
- Understanding yeast as the catalyst to brewing
- Adding fruit, spice, and adjuncts

Beer is alive. And as a living entity, it grows and changes over time while remaining true to its original being. What grows and changes with beer has much to do with ingredients and craft, location, climate, cycling of grains, and water conditions. But what truly keeps beer alive is the human passion for quality of life. In this chapter, you will learn about the four essential ingredients found in beer, as well as a few other items that you can add—including passion.

As you read about the four basic ingredients you truly gain respect for how such a limited ingredient list can yield hundreds of different layers of taste. And learning about the qualities of each ingredient gives you a leg-up for discerning those layers of taste when you sip a brew.

# The Essential Ingredients in Beer

Nearly every type of beer has four basic raw ingredients:

- Water

- Malt, also known as fermentable sugars (remember, it began with malted barley, still most used by brewers)

- Hops

- Yeast

A brewer creates a recipe as does any cook or baker, combining specific amounts of each ingredient to produce a desired color, aroma, taste, flavor, alcohol level, and feeling of balance. Slight changes in quantity alter any or every aspect. It's the same with beer as it is with cookies. Chocolate chip cookies change with the use of dark, sweet, or white chips; large chunks or small bits; bleached white flour or unbleached flour; the addition of oatmeal; applesauce replacing oil; and length of time baked. Beer tastes are akin to the differing tastes from changes in a basic cookie recipe.

It's the same with beer when it comes to location of brewing. The beer from your local brewpub, tapped just at its prime and served fresh on-site is close to being home-baked and out of the oven. Buying beer in a growler to take home or freshly bottled or canned beer on-site at the brewery is akin to cookies baked at the store and bought fresh that day.

Canned or bottled beer shipped to a store from a local brewer is expected to be somewhat fresher than is a brew from a production brewery farther away. Like cookies, Craft beers have a shelf life and brewers mark the date of the brew or indicate "Best Used By" on the label. We know that some cookies taste fine even after the expiration date; it's the same with beer. Always check with the sales clerk to learn how long that particular beer can be stored in the refrigerator or other cool place away from light.

# Water

Water has localized factors: it can be hard or soft, with gradations in between. Where it originates and what it flows through dictates its qualities, which, in turn, can dictate the best style of beer to brew.

**BREW WATCH**

Specific locations are known for the beer they brew because of the water. We talk more about that in Chapter 6 when we get to the nitty-gritty of categories or classes and styles.

Brewers pay close attention to the source and quality of the water they use because water constitutes 90 percent of a beer. Here are two important rules to remember:

> #1: The water has to be free from contamination of any kind.

> #2: The water has to be suitable for the brewing process.

Distilled water is not an option. The qualities that make it great for your steam iron or humidifier inhibit the work of enzymes and yeast.

Purified water with all the right amount of salts is an option. Tap water, however, is used most often. While some aspects of water from your tap are best removed—chlorine, sulfur, and iron will ruin the taste of beer—the brewing process needs calcium as a yeast nutrient and for beer to mature to be just right for drinking. If the required level of calcium isn't naturally available, brewers add gypsum and calcium carbonate.

Plzen, in the Czech Republic, reportedly has the softest water known. The Pilsner-style Lagers brewed there are world renowned for their distinctive taste credited to the water—delivering a malty *mouthfeel* despite the high hopping rate.

**DEFINITIONS**

The **mouthfeel** is how the beer feels in the mouth. Is might be full or thin; dry, bitter, or sweet; smooth or creamy.

On the other hand, the English town of Burton-on-Trent has water with a high mineral content (especially calcium sulphate) and also earns a hallowed place in the storied history of clear, bright bitters. In the nineteenth century, the town was hailed as "the town of brewers." Its legacy now resides in pale Ales brewed and enjoyed elsewhere because brewers "Burtonize" their available water by adding gypsum salts.

Brewers test the water available for their use to determine water quality. The rule of thumb is: softer waters are better for Lagers and darker Ales, and harder waters are better for pale Ales with more hop presence, possibly because the calcium increases the quantity of malt during the mashing stage. A beer needs a high malt backbone to support a large amount of hops.

But water for breweries extends beyond the brewpot. For every gallon of water mixed with malt to start the brewing process, a brewery uses 5 additional gallons to keep the operation sparkling clean and to cool the brews. Most breweries today utilize sustainable systems to recycle and reclaim water from cleaning and cooling. (Note that the malting process also requires a fair amount of water, as we explain in the next section.)

# Malt

While water is the spirit of beer, malt supplies its body and soul. Just as water needs to have the right quality and quantity of salts for effective brewing, grains need to have certain qualities undergo altered states to serve well as malt. Barley was the original grain used in brewing because it was plentiful in the Fertile Crescent. In regions where wheat is more plentiful it is the grain of choice. Rye and corn along with barley and wheat also are used for some brewing.

Barley is the preferred grain (sometimes referred to as cereal) because it provides the best extraction rate of sugars. And as with water, there are preferred varieties. For best results, brewers want barley that's low in nitrogen with plump, sound grains that will germinate at an even rate. Barley was not native to the North American continent. Barley production was introduced in the United States in the seventeenth century by Europeans. Geographic and climatic conditions, plus genetics, altered some characteristics of the grain. Thus, beers brewed in the United States and Canada are distinctive from barley brews elsewhere. And while two-row barley is preferred worldwide, the macrobrewers in the United States prefer six-row barley, which is more cost effective to grow.

Wheat malts require extra care because they are smaller in kernel size than are barley malts. Brewers will use from 5 to 70 percent of wheat for a brew, adding barley for the rest of the bill. There are several types of wheat malts, including white wheat, red wheat, pale wheat, cara wheat, and chocolate wheat. Because wheat has no outer husk, it has fewer tannins than barley. Wheat contributes more protein to a beer and is responsible for a fluff head and longer head retention.

Wheat is what makes German Wheat beers special. Wheat lends a lighter flavor. The lightest flavors come from corn and rice. Oatmeal provides a specialty beer.

Rye malt is even smaller than wheat malt, posing even more problems for the brewer in the malting process. *Malsters* and brewers figure out ways to cope with the challenges. Rye is known for giving beer a spicy or sour-like quality. Think of the taste of rye bread.

 **DEFINITIONS**

A **malster** is the person who transforms barley seeds into malt for brewing.

## The Malting Process

Grains require a bit of magic to become useful ingredients for brewing. It's a universal malting process with master malsters in charge. While mechanization has replaced the traditional floor malting procedure, the steps remain as follows:

1.  Remove the straw and dirt from the freshly harvested grains.

2.  Dry the grains to reduce the moisture and enable the grain to be stored without getting moldy.

3.  Soak the grains in water. Alternate between steeping the grains in the water and draining the water for about three days.

4.  To begin germination, the damp grain is spread out and the seeds are allowed to sprout and grow over five days. This creates the sugars required for brewing. Germinating grains have to be raked and turned over at least three times a day so they don't mat up.

5.  To halt germination, this "green malt" is baked in a kiln at high temperatures for at least two days. The exact temperature determines the type of malt, from very light to very dark. Higher temperatures yield darker colors and stronger flavors. Brewers might use one malt by itself or blend different malts in varying measurements to produce the exact kind of beer they want.

The best way to obtain malted barley, wheat, and rye is to visit a homebrew shop or a brewpub or brewery and ask for a few grains of each. Visiting a homebrew shop will also give you background on the art and craft of a malster.

The miracle of malting is not in transformation of appearance—the malted grain doesn't look that much different from the freshly harvested grain. The magic is in texture and taste. Try it. Gingerly bite on a raw barley grain—it's hard and dangerously able to harm a tooth, and it doesn't have much flavor. After five malting steps, try the barley again. Now the grain is nice to eat, crunchy, and nutty.

## Go Where the Grain Is

In the United States, North Dakota and Minnesota produce the majority of the six-row malting barley, followed by South Dakota and Idaho. Montana, Idaho, Washington, Colorado, and Wyoming lead in two-row barley production. It follows, therefore, that large malting operations are close to where barley is grown. However, globalization has affected the malting industry. Malt company directories show that it's just as likely for a brewery to obtain malt from overseas as from across the United States. Thus, grains could be coming from anyplace and everyplace, because the dominant companies buy grain at international markets.

In counterbalance, with the advance of sustainable practices, breweries have begun to look for malsters closer to home. In a way, this is taking a page from the macrobrewer's business plan. Macrobrewers contract with grain producers and malsters, as well as with hops growers, to ensure they have a supply of ingredients according to company specifications. Of course, being big means a company can negotiate costs to keep prices low.

Because microbrewers are not in a position to buy grains in huge quantities and thus earn discounts, they pay more per unit than do the macrobrewers. One way to mitigate this is for brewers in a particular area to order together and earn a discount for the larger quantity thus cutting each individual brewery's cost. However, the up-side of this is that by requiring a lower quantity, microbrewers can choose to use unique barley grains with flavors emanating from local terrain.

As small and local malting operations appear all over North America, we are witnessing a revival of distinctive heirloom barley and wheat grains that are capable of imparting long-forgotten flavors and aromas to beer. The overall intent is three-fold:

- To decrease the imprint on Earth by decreasing the use of fossil fuels

- To increase freshness and quality

- To turn the microbrewing industry more toward malt and away from the current trend of hop-heavy pale Ales

Micromalsters laud malt's sweet character as a distinctive taste profile for Craft beer.

Malster Glenn Roberts, founder of Anson Mills in Columbia, South Carolina, is known as a leader in the movement toward artisan grain growers. He makes the point that the future of brewing is having "total control over ingredients." The challenge is in staying cost effective. Small usually means higher cost, so the consumer has to be willing to pay more for local.

The emerging combined micromalting and localized barley-growing industry celebrates its pioneers in the same way microbrewers celebrate their pioneers. Micromalters and the heirloom and small local barley growers are developing support groups to help each other learn the craft and art that largely was lost when Prohibition shut down local malting operations and, thus, the need for local barley producers.

Most micromalters, like microbrewers, start with a homemade system that is labor and time intensive, but all claim it's worth the effort. A computer search for micromalters and small barley producers brings up a bevy of inspiring stories. Barley malt as a multifaceted *body and soul* commodity now is poised to push the envelope in the direction of balance, "partnering with" rather than being "overridden by" hops. Begin to look for new styles with "sweet and crisp" descriptions as the trend continues to bring us back to the beginning.

**DEFINITIONS**

Malt is referred to as a **body and soul** commodity because it is the backbone of a brew, second to water in quantity used for the brewing process. With the emerging micromalster movement "body and soul" reflects a sustainable culture concept emphasizing a local and minimal imprint on Earth.

# Hops

If water provides beer's spirit, and malt its body and soul, then beer's zing springs from hops. Hops are a flowering vine. The oil of the flowers adds flavor (this is the category of bittering hops) or aroma (aroma hops). Brewers can use a single hop or a mixture to create a specific taste and aroma profile.

Beer without hops lacks longevity; it has to be drunk soon after brewing. Hops also provide clarity of color, which promotes good head retention, stabilizing flavor, and cleansing the palate from excessive malt sweetness. And last, but not least, hops seem to be able to partner with malt and yeast to provide a virtual rainbow of flavors, including citrusy, spicy, floral, and herbal.

**BREW WATCH**

Hops are a later addition to the making of beer and are somewhat fraught with controversy. One could spend quite a bit of barstool time traversing the topic of hops—why its use was not originally favored, why its use became a power struggle, why hops now are a favored ingredient, and more. To sort out fact and inconsistencies repeated over centuries, check out beer writer Martyn Cornell's blog and/or website. He attempts to sort out the swirl around hops with careful research.

## How Hops Are Used

We don't know exactly when and where hops use originated. We only know that it became accepted as both an alternative to and an additional part of the earlier spice bundle. The spice bundle itself was controversial because some combinations were unsafe and some were unscrupulous, used to increase the volume but not the quality of beer. Thus, to establish purity and safety, the Reinheitsgebot, or "German Purity Law," came into effect in 1516, establishing that only water, barley, and hops could be used in making beer. Note that yeast was not listed; at that time, yeast was not known as an ingredient. The cause of fermentation was accepted as something that happened spontaneously. (More about yeast comes in the section appropriately titled "Yeast.")

Hops grow on a vine as conelike flowers that yield a complex oil. Hops plants grow in the wild and are domesticated to specifically add aroma, flavor, and bitterness. As the palate of consumers has widened toward greater degrees of bitterness, growers have developed hops with higher alpha acids to provide more bitterness. As with malt, hops can be used singly or in combinations to gain the exact taste profile a brewer wants. Brewers rely on charts to determine qualities of bittering, flavor, and aroma found in each brand of hops.

Brewers call the process of adding hops for flavor and aroma finishing, or conditioning. Thus, these hops are called aromatic or finishing hops. They retain their aroma during the boil. On the other hand, bittering hops lose their aroma during the boiling process. A handful of hops have the capacity to retain aroma during the boil and provide bittering, including Cascade, Centennial, Columbus, Northern Brewer, and Warrior.

Aroma hops that you'll most often see listed with Craft beer ingredients include Crystal, Fuggles, Goldings, Mount Hood, Perle, Saaz, and Willamette. High alpha bittering varieties most often listed are Chinook, Cluster, Eroica, Galena, and Nugget. Learn about the special qualities of each hops variety by talking with brewers and asking them why they choose certain combinations or favor a specific variety.

## Where to Find Quality Hops

Certain regions of the world are renowned for their quality of hops because they are located between latitudes 35° and 55°, either north or south of the equator. Yields are principally affected by day length during the growing season. Germany produces the most hops, with the United States coming in second.

**BREW WATCH**

The Pacific Northwest leads the production of hops in the United States. Idaho has two vibrant hops-growing regions. Anheuser-Busch even owns and operates a 1,700-acre hops farm in the northwest corner of Idaho.

It's fun to look at a world globe and locate the other major hops regions between latitudes 35° and 55°, including China, Czech Republic, Poland, Slovenia, Democratic People's Republic of Korea, United Kingdom, and Albania. Hops nevertheless can grow any place where they are nurtured, and many Craft breweries plant some for their signature fall seasonal beers. However, growing hops presents a challenge because they need special soils to root deeply. In addition, the vines grow higher than any human can reach without ladders and are susceptible to blight.

Harvested hops are gently dried in kilns and then placed into sacks for delivery to breweries for fresh hopping. However, most of the hop harvest is further processed, to permit longer shelf life. Pressed into pellets, hops last until the next harvest.

**BREW WATCH**

The Flanders City of Poperinge might have the most interesting story about becoming a center for hops production. According to local lore, Poperinge originally was famous for the cloth its citizens wove. However, in 1322, the nearby City of Ypres sought and got exclusive cloth-weaving rights from the ruling Count Louis of Nevers. With that edict, the people of Poperinge were without a means of support. So they turned to growing hops and became so expert at it that Poperinge hops were sought after throughout Europe. In 2007, during a visit to Poperinge at the time of the hops harvest, I also learned about how Poperinge hops production survived the religious wars of the sixteenth century and the devastation of World Wars I and II. So we toasted the tenacity of the citizenry across centuries with the golden-hued Poperinge Hommel Ale from the Brewery Van Eecke. Michael Jackson's description is enough to lure one to taste and toast: "A roselike flow-eriness, honeyish notes, orange-zest hop flavors and a late spicy, cuminseed dryness." It's especially suited to pair with spicy foods.

# Yeast

Yeast is the catalyst for brewing—without it, you have gruel. Yeast is the zesty component that transforms water, malt, and hops into an alcoholic beverage. Yet yeast remained a mystery until 1857, when Louis Pasteur identified yeast as a living organism and described its role in fermentation. Through his experiments and evaluations, he was able to identify, isolate, and remove contaminants that caused problems in brewing. Nevertheless, yeast remains unpredictable, with a life of its own. However, having some control over yeast and fermentation has revolutionized the brewing of beer (and the baking of bread), with the exception of some Belgian brewers, who continue to utilize natural, airborne yeasts to inoculate the brew for their specialty sour beers.

Two hundred years earlier, in 1685 Holland, a scientist named Leeuwenhoek was the first to describe the "appearance" of yeast, but he had not worked out its function so it was of little help to brewers because they still didn't fully understand how it worked.

Pasteur started his yeast quest in 1871 in France, and his work found an advocate in Denmark. Thus, yeast "taming" became a multinational enterprise with the opening of a laboratory at Copenhagen's Carlsberg Brewery by owner J. C. Jacobsen, allowing Emil Hansen to further Pasteur's research by breaking down yeast to single strains. Here finally was real help for brewers. Even though predictability is greater with single-strain yeast, many brewers still utilize multiple yeast strains for special results. Basically, each brewery develops its house yeast or yeasts for top-fermenting Ales and bottom-fermenting Lagers. Some new yeast strains work for both, and some are developed for hybrids of Ales and Lagers.

Since 1871 enterprising chemists have developed strains of yeast for brewing, especially marketing brewer's yeast for homebrewers and commercial brewers. There now are many choices for a brewer, suited to different styles.

With the advent of the European Union, the Provisional German Beer Law replaced the Reinheitsgebot (1988), to now allow yeast along with wheat malt and cane sugar in the making of beer to meet the strict German industry standards.

The workings of yeast continue to intrigue scientists. The question "How did Lager beer come to be?" has fueled a series of research projects. In August 2011, a report issued by a team engaged in "a five-year search around the world" identified a species of wild yeast that lives on beech trees in the forests of Argentina. That led to pondering how a yeast native to Argentina made its way to Germany and led the way to the invention of bottom-fermenting beer 600 years ago, further revolutionizing the brewing industry.

## Fermentation of Yeast

The initial yeast fermentation method was wild or spontaneous. The grains (sugar supply) were steeped in water and left out in the open for "nature" to do its part. With the development of yeasts in laboratories, now they are packaged in pressed cakes, sprinkles, or liquid form.

For brewing, there are two kinds of yeast:

- Yeast fermenting at warm temperatures (Ales, Porters, Stouts, Altbier, Kolsch, and Wheat beer)

- Yeast fermenting at cool or cold temperatures (Pilsners, Dortmunders, Märzen, Bocks, and American Malt Liquors)

Warm fermenting makes Ales; cold fermenting makes Lagers. Both warm and cold fermentation can take place in open or closed vessels. Open fermentation never requires covering to ward off contamination and unwanted stuff falling in. Closed fermentation is more controlled in a contamination-free vessel that can be monitored for the length of fermentation. A secondary fermentation can take place in casks (barrels) at the brewers, or in the bottle or can while the beer is waiting to be opened and poured.

# Passion As an "Ingredient"

Passion is as much an ingredient as water, malt, hops, and yeast. Passion is the shared element that keeps a brewer coming back every morning to scrub every inch of the brewery and every vessel and container and measuring implement, to stand on a water-splotched concrete floor in knee-high boots, to wear a wool hat over a steaming kettle and strain the muscles paddling the brew while balancing on a ladder.

Ninety percent of brewing is cleaning and physical grunt work. You have to love it every bit as much as ballet dancers love their art and craft. Brewing is 24/7 times 52. Taking a day or a week off means double duty ahead of time to prepare sufficient stock. Only if the operation is big enough to have multiple brewers is there such a thing as a two-week vacation without a guilty conscience. And even then, 9 times out of 10, it's a brewer's holiday of visiting other breweries. Ask a brewer about vacations and order two beers.

By now, you've figured out that brewers are into discovery, invention, and innovation, which brings us to "anything goes," even if it's a one-time event.

# Adding Flavoring with Fruits and Spices

While you can't make beer without the four basic ingredients, you're not restricted to only those four. This has been the case for centuries. Fruit beers are synonymous with Belgian Abbey brews, particularly cherries for Kriek and raspberries for Frambozen. These fruits add a secondary fermentation for a truly unique and acquired taste profile.

In the United States, apples from the fall harvest are favorites in beer and add a dimension beyond cider. Pumpkin beers are expected every fall. And lately, the pepper phenomenon has paired with beers for flavorings from every hue and shape. Orange and lemon peel spark a line of beers to pair with cheese and desserts. But it's not just fruits and vegetables.

Flavoring with herbs and spices has been revived from ancient traditions. Honey has held its own from the beginning of brewing on the African continent, the place of origin for honey as well as beer. As flavor enhancers, these additions might raise the cost of making a brew, but their popularity offsets the price point variance. Brewers who use flavor enhancers are careful to point out that theirs is an "all-malt" beer.

# Adding Adjuncts

Adjuncts have come to mean a way to save money, to make up for the availability of barley or wheat, and/or to "lighten" a beer to appeal to people who do not want a full-bodied taste profile. Here is a list of some of the most common adjuncts:

- Some brewers add sugar to replace the more expensive barley and/or wheat malt. While it ferments quickly and adds alcohol, sugar does not offer the body—the backbone—that barley and wheat malt provide. Thus, the beer has alcohol without the balance.

- Sometimes heated sugars are used to darken beers in place of using darker barley malts. This is a taste preference sometimes found in Belgian recipes.

- Macrobreweries in the United States are known to use half flaked corn and half barley malt to produce a beer that is much drier than an all-barley beer. Its color is also lighter, as is its taste profile. Rice as an adjunct provides a light, crisp finish and is the earmark of Anheuser-Busch beers.

Brewers love to experiment with different grain possibilities even if they present new challenges. Three commonalities include:

- Popped popcorn is added for head retention. Some Craft brewers create this as a specialty brew.

- Unmalted barley gives beer a black color and a bitter flavor. Used sparingly as Guinness does, unmalted barley creates a truly distinctive profile.

- Malt extracts are often used by beginning homebrewers, who then move into all-grain as they gain expertise and have time for that extra step required with all-grain.

# Pushing the Alcohol Envelope

West Coast brewers with an abundance of hops at their doorstep have largely been responsible for the hoppier beers that now are widespread throughout the United States. The hop-head generation tends to cluster around the beer with the next-highest alcohol and hop content. These levels are measured precisely by industry standards. Every beer has an alcohol by volume (ABV) and international bittering unit (IBU) percent designation, as required by law.

The higher the ABV number, the more alcohol is in the beer, thus the more likely you need to be aware of how much you are drinking and how well you can handle that much alcohol in your system and stay sober. One must be cognizant of alcohol levels and personal abilities to handle alcohol. Some high-alcohol beers can be deceptively smooth so awareness up front is primary.

The higher the IBU number, the more hops in the beer, thus the more bitterness. But one cannot go by numbers alone. A beer made with a lot of malt can balance out the bitterness of hops. People who favor bitterness in beer best enjoy India Pale Ales and Imperial IPAs. People who do not like bitter beers favor Stouts, with a malt sweetness that is balanced by a lesser amount of hops bitterness.

For a number of years, the race has been on between brewers to brew beers with more alcohol and more hops, but there's a noticeable swing back to "session beers" with moderate alcohol and bitterness content. The idea here is to allow a person to enjoy more than one beer at a session, or during an evening or mealtime. Session beers are fully flavored and carefully balanced.

The conversation among brewers sometimes ventures toward, "Are some of us hiding not-well-made beer with the addition of hops?" Or, "You know, it's easier to make a hoppy beer than a balanced beer." Or, "After burning your palate on an overdose of hops, how can you enjoy food?"

So, gentle reader, the question of content and context rests with you. Brewers are in the business to make ends meet. They brew what you and I put money down for. As with the similarly burgeoning coffee and tea industries, variety, distinction, and quality are requirements as consumers become savvy and expect nothing short of excellence every time.

## The Least You Need to Know

- Brewing is an ongoing process of change and innovation as brewers over centuries have striven to do more with less—that is, tease as many different layers of flavors from just four basic ingredients.

- Beer requires four essential ingredients: water, malted barley or wheat, hops and yeast. Along with how much of each ingredient, the brewer has to be cognizant of the condition of the water, the art and craft of the malting process, the dynamics of different yeast strains, and the qualities of diverse hop brands.

- Consumers dictate the menu of beers. Professional brewing is a business. People drink the beer that pleases their palate. Some brewers cater to a specific audience, some welcome a wide range of preferences. Ultimately, a beer that sells itself is brewed again.

# The Brewing Processes

## In This Chapter

- Reviewing different types of breweries
- Understanding how brewing becomes Craft
- An example Craft brewery production facility

Beer is universal, having appeared early in just about every culture on every continent. Yet it is local, with a taste profile linked to the specifics of geography, climate, available ingredients, and methods of brewing. Beer can be made in a totally hands-on method, utilizing pots and buckets in your kitchen, or can be technologically produced, in tuns and tanks in a specially outfitted building.

This chapter introduces you to the brewing process so that you understand some of the terminology you'll encounter as you learn more about tasting beer.

# Various Types of Breweries

The modern era beer industry reflects multiple levels of brewing for private and public use including homebrewers, some of whom venture forth to open a production brewery, brewpub, gastropub, brewery with a full service restaurant, or a brewery with a beer garden (based on the concept of Craft brewing). Each option is surrounded by a network of supporting and supportive components, some evident, some not so evident. In the space we have we can't touch on the totality of the swirl of activity that makes up the brewing industry, but we hope to get you curious enough to want to investigate on your own by visiting breweries and asking questions.

**BREW WATCH**

Beer is capable of being hugely diverse and varied and yet can be manipulated to become virtually bland with no peaks and valleys of taste. Beer can be elevating or debilitating based on quantity of consumption. Beer can bring people together or split them apart according to personal philosophy.

Here are some general descriptions of different types of breweries:

- Production breweries brew beer to be sold off the premises. Some production breweries have a tasting room and also offer tours. Food is not served.

- Brewpubs brew beer to be sold on the premises along with food. Pub food is usually simple and predictable based on the location. Most brewpubs will fill growlers for take-out. Some brewpubs also bottle or can and fill kegs for sale off premises.

- Gastropubs brew beer to be sold on the premises, but the concept of food is referred to as "cuisine," usually reflecting a particular culture, such as a Belgian Gastropub.

- Breweries with a beer garden make their beer mainly to be sold off the premises. They also sell pints on premise to be enjoyed in a space outside the brewery, with some food service catered or brought in. However, some brewpubs also have outside seating areas sometimes referred to as their beer garden.

- Breweries with a full service restaurant are larger than a brewpub and have a more extensive menu; they might be separated from the brewery itself.

- Commercial breweries are sometimes referred to as "macro-breweries" because of the volume of beer brewed on a daily, monthly, and yearly basis. They do not fit into the Brewers Association guidelines as a Craft brewery.

Professional brewers and owners of breweries on all levels need to be aware of all aspects associated with running a business. For example, they must keep track of trends in marketing and research that relate to consumer preferences and also must stay abreast of all aspects connected with the ingredients of beer. These include the growing, harvesting, and processing of grains and hops; water quality; and yeast.

Brewers are avid readers of research bulletins and trade journals. They attend conferences and enroll in workshops to gain cutting-edge information about every aspect of brewing, from accounting to *zymurgy*. In addition, brewers develop a personal relationship with malsters, hop growers and suppliers, and yeast companies. They frequently travel from their home breweries to visit their suppliers on-site.

**DEFINITIONS**

Originating with Louis Pasteur's laboratory work concerning yeast and fermentation, and thus confined to the science of fermentation, **zymurgy** has become a generic term to describe the process of brewing beer.

# Brewing as Craft

Some people acquire artistry through study and practice; some are simply born with a gift that gets perfected with the doing. The brewing process is intricate, requiring careful observation of nature and attention to detail.

Timing is of the essence, and there's no such thing as a small part in the brewing process. The following is a general description of the brewing process:

1.  Mill your own barley, or buy malted grain.

2.  Mash up the barley malt or wheat grains.

3.  Place it in water.

4.  Boil.

5.  Cool.

6.  Separate the spent grains from the liquid that now contains the grain nutrients.

 **BREW WATCH**

A tour at a major brewery brings you into the process that began in 1876 when Adolphus Busch perfected the recipe, the brewing process, and the taste of the American-style Lager. Under the heading "Brewing brings together art and science," the tour shows us that "[w]hile brewing technology has improved over the years, the 7-step process and the brewmaster's role have stood the test of time."

7.  Pitch in hops.

8.  Add yeast.

9.  Pitch in more hops, if desired.

10. Store in a container away from light of any kind.

11. Test periodically.

12. Tap and drink when it tastes just right.

How much of each ingredient, when, and for how long? And "just right" to one person can be completely different from what's "just right" to the next person. So what is "just right" to a brewer? This is where art interweaves with craft and science.

# Brewing at a Craft Brewery

Here's a thumbnail run-down of the steps from Craft brewer to you:

1. Milling: Crack the malt husks to expose the grain's starches, then drop the grist into the hopper.

2. Mashing: Mix the grist with water and boil and stir in the mash tun for an hour and a half.

3. Lautering: Separate the liquid wort from the grains, rinse all leftover grain particles into the lauter tun, then strain the spent grains from the liquid wort.

4. Boiling: Move the wort to the brew kettle and boil for one to two hours; add hops.

5. Cooling: Before adding yeast, the wort has to be quickly cooled to the precise temperature for yeast to work.

6. Fermenting: Pitch the yeast into the cooled wort (top-fermenting yeast for Ales, bottom-fermenting yeast for Lagers); keep the wort in fermenters for 4-8 days.

7. Conditioning: Pump the fermented wort into conditioning tanks where the temperature drops to near-freezing so the yeast goes dormant; this lasts 10-30 days. (Some brews are transferred to Brite/Bright tanks for the introduction of carbonation.)

8. Quality control.

9. Bottling/canning/kegging.

10. Packaging/shipping.

A more lengthy description follows in the section "Production Facilities at a Craft Brewery."

## Upland Brewing Company: An Example of Craft

Upland Brewing Company in Bloomington, Indiana, is both typical and atypical as a Craft brewery. It started as a brewpub in 1998 and grew into a production brewery. In 2013, it expanded its facility. This is part of the brewery's story, as related by owner Doug Dayhoff:

> Many of our brews are unique twists on traditional recipes, while others are products of our own imaginations. We're proud to say that several of our beers have brought home national and international medals and awards, but what we really care about is brewing the kinds of beer we like to drink, and providing a fresh local option to our communities. It never hurts to get a pat on the back, though! Along the way, we've made lots of friends and drank our unfair share of good beer, all while trying to do good in our communities and do well as a Craft brewery.

> The name *Upland* comes from the Norman and Crawford Uplands, the term geologists gave to our area of southern Indiana, which was never overrun by the glaciers that flattened much of Indiana's landscape. The raised highlands, or "uplands," remained untouched, resulting in a region of rugged, heavily wooded hills and hollows. The land was beautiful but poor, and life was not easy for early settlers. This adversity bred independent thinkers who had strong wills, a connection to the land, and a wry sense of humor about life. Our approach to brewing beer honors the spirit of these people and this place.

Upland is typical of Craft breweries, with its sense of place and affinity for civic concern. Dayhoff says,

> In a world increasingly dominated by giant multinational companies, foods processed from bits and pieces of unknowable "stuff" collected from around the globe, and mass-marketed entertainment, we think it's more important

than ever to keep our local communities, cultures, and economies strong. That's why we source ingredients and materials used in the brewery and the Tap Room locally whenever possible, eat at local restaurants, support local musicians and artists, and help raise money for local not-for-profits.

We also strive to minimize our impact on the beautiful land we call home by conserving energy in the brewery and utilizing a solar water heating system. Every fall, the brewery hosts the Hillbilly Haiku Americana Concert, bringing in local, regional, and national touring musicians for an outdoor concert to raise money for Sycamore Land Trust. We also donate a percentage of the profit from every keg of Preservation Pilsner to a land trust in the area where the keg was tapped.

We visited Upland Brewery with its three levels of brewing capacity. The original brewery that is part of the brewpub now is dedicated to Upland's Specialty Sours. The new production facility also provides space for recipe design on what is essentially a homebrew setup. The Head Brewer showed us around the "old" brewery as he was "firing up" to brew Sours.

Upland is testing a new recipe designed by Assistant Brewers and *Cellarpersons* that they hope will become an Upland Spring Seasonal. The Head Brewer helps them scale the recipe from the 10-gallon homebrew system to a full production batch. Scaling up a recipe from a little under a ½-barrel batch to a 37-barrel batch volume is an act of precision combined with familiarity, as unique brewing systems have individual eccentricities and efficiencies. Drawing out similar specifications and flavor profiles from pilot brews to larger systems requires understanding the mechanics of both brewing systems and how they function with regard to ingredients. Brewers take into account as many data points as possible when pilot brewing recipes to accurately replicate and potentially improve the beer when scaling into a larger volume format.

> **DEFINITIONS**
>
> A **Cellarperson** (*Cellarman* was the original terminology) tradition-
> ally is the person in charge of the alcohol supply in a bar or restaurant.
> In brewing terminology, *Cellarman* refers to the person who looks
> after the beer as it is brewing, making sure to follow the Head Brewer's
> instructions for monitoring the tanks along the steps during the brew-
> ing process; this person is responsible for maintaining the highest
> qualities of cleanliness in every phase of brewing. *Cellaring* is the term
> for storing alcoholic beverages.

## Production Facilities at a Craft Brewery

We took a step-by-step tour of the new Upland Brewing Company
production facility. What follows is a detailed description of how
they produce a Craft beer.

Production at Upland Brewing Company starts with the cellar
schedule, which is a daily, weekly, and monthly listing of everyone's
job and unassigned projects. The brewing term "cellar" goes back to
the job of keeping track of the stock and making timely deliveries. It
has expanded to include the general grunt work of keeping track of
everything in a timely fashion.

People aspiring to become brewers in a production brewery or a
brewpub begin as Cellarmen/woman, thus learning from the bottom
up through the traditional Guild System, the basis of becoming a
Brewmaster. Cleaning is a Cellarman/assistant brewer's constant
chore. Everything is washed squeaky clean before and after use,
including the boil kettle with its percolator and the hop kettle.

Different kinds of malt are required to provide each style of beer
with the exact characteristics desired. Most Craft breweries buy their
malted barley and wheat from companies specializing in malting
grain. Mass production breweries usually operate their own malting
facility. The advantage to buying malt in bulk is reduced cost. A bulk
delivery every other month costs less over a year than do shipments
of bags of malt; over time, the cost of installing silos pays for itself.
A brewery needs to use sufficient quantities of malt (six- to eight-
week turnover) to ensure the malt is fresh.

**BREW WATCH**

Some brews require smaller quantities of specialty malt, as in this case when the brew requires specially roasted caramel malt. The bags of malt are carefully stored on pallets off the floor. Hops and hop pellets are stored in a specially refrigerated room.

Malt from a silo is piped down to the grain mill. The exact quantities of each type of malt are fed into the mill. Milling means cracking or crushing the malted grain to expose the starches in each grain. Great care is taken to break the grain while retaining much of the husk. This is essential for the grain to absorb the water it is mixed with, in the mashing step, and to retain the best taste provided by the husk. Milled grain is called grist. The milled grain/grist is then sent to the milled grain hopper, also referred to as the grist hopper.

From the grain/grist hopper, the grist is moved through the grain auger transfer into a Steele'e Masher, a device that keeps the grist from forming into clumps when it falls into the water in the mash tun. The water temperature must be kept precisely right to activate the enzymes for fermentable sugar.

The mixture of grist and water is recirculated in the mash tun for about an hour and a half. The liquid is called the wort (pre-fermented beer) that is separated from the malt grain. Any remaining grain particles are then rinsed into the lauter-tun by a process brewers call sparging. To ensure removal of any leftover elements not wanted in the final brew, brewers strain the wort. This process is called lautering.

The next step is boiling in the boil/brew kettle with a percolator. The wort is boiled for one to two hours, depending on the style of beer. Hops are added at specific times during the boil in accordance to the desired aroma and bitterness of the style.

A hopback provides a way to add hops for maximum retention of the volatile hop aroma compounds that would be killed by the hot wort. A hopback is a sealed chamber placed between the brew kettle and the wort chiller. So instead of hops being dropped into the boil kettle, hops are put into the hopback; hot wort from the boil kettle is run through the hopback and immediately cooled in the wort chiller before being sent to the whirlpool/chiller.

The wort is then transferred from the boil kettle to the whirlpool/chiller. It is essential to quickly get the liquid at the precise temperature to introduce yeast and start fermentation.

Hot liquor and cold liquor tanks are brewer terms for hot water and cold water tanks. Hot liquor tanks are buffer tanks with hot water that is used during lautering to sparge the grain bed (get all the sugar out of the malt left behind). Cold liquor tanks are buffer tanks with cold water used to cool the hot wort (to which hops have been added) so yeast can be added to the wort for fermentation to begin.

Fermenters are large storage tanks for the wort to become beer. Grundy tanks are smaller tanks. "Grundy" is the term that American brewers use for these tanks (originated in the U.K. where they are used as pub cellar tanks to directly dispense carbonated beers from pub cellars). Both tanks can be utilized beyond fermentation for the processes of conditioning and as a substitute for a bright tank for carbonation. Glycol lines provide a state-of-the art cooling system.

Filtering is an additional step to "stabilize the beer," which means to remove bits of yeast and give the beer a clear, brilliant, shiny look. Most times brewers do not filter and instead rely on the natural settling to the bottom of the bottle or can or keg of any particles of yeast that did not settle during the process of fermentation. Filtered beer is usually held in a bright tank before being bottled/kegged/canned.

Nothing leaves the building before being checked in the quality lab. Consistency with quality and safety are the mantra for brewers.

## The Least You Need to Know

- The modern era beer industry reflects multiple levels of brewing for private and public use including homebrewers, production breweries, brewpubs, gastropubs, breweries with a full service restaurant, or a brewery with a beer garden (based on the concept of Craft brewing).

- In a beer recipe, "just right" to one person can be completely different from what's "just right" to the next person. Brewers interweave art with craft and science to get their beers "just right."

- Drawing out similar specifications and flavor profiles from pilot brews to larger systems requires understanding the mechanics of both brewing systems and how they function with regard to ingredients.

# The Basic Styles

## In This Chapter

- Top-fermenting classical-style Ales
- Bottom-fermenting classical-style Lagers
- The various types of Wheat beers

The Craft beer industry embraces the tradition of classical beer styles. That's where a brewer starts and remains centered. Brewers strive for quality and consistency at all levels, while also engaging in innovation to expand a style and conducting research to bring back an ancient brew. In Chapter 2, we explored the influences from diverse regions of the world and touched on the unique contributions made by brewers in the United States. In this chapter, we concentrate on the different beers within each style that you are most likely to find in any brewpub or bottled and canned by any production brewery.

# Classical Beer Styles

"Style" in beer refers to a specific set of ingredients and balance between these ingredients. For example, Pale Ale is a style in the Ale category; Pale Lager is a style in the Lager category. In his benchmark book, *The World Guide to Beer*, great beer writer Michael Jackson introduced the classical beer styles as falling into three broad categories:

- Made with barley malt, top-fermented (Ales)

- Brewed with barley malt, bottom-fermented (Lagers)

- Brewed with barley malt and some wheat, and also top-fermented (Wheats, as categorized in this chapter)

The first thing to consider about terminology is how loosely words are used. Jackson points out, for instance, that in Britain and the United States, *Lager* has become generic for the macroproduced, bottom-fermented beverages that he says are, "loose local interpretations of the Pilsner style." In England, *Ale* has been the "generic term for English-style top-fermented beers; usually copper-colored, but sometimes darker."

Ale is the oldest beer category, stemming from the first brew discovered in Mesopotamia. It is referred to as "top fermented" because the yeast rises to the top as it works. Lagers, as we know them today, were invented in Bavaria in the early nineteenth century when brewers experimented with brewing in ice-filled mountain caves as a way to prolong their shelf life. During the longer brewing process, the yeast (and other solids) settled to the bottom of the barrel. Thus, Lagers are referred to as "bottom fermented." Even though Wheat beers are grouped in a class by themselves, they are top fermented and, thus, rightfully part of the Ale category.

**BREW WATCH**

Yeast, for fermentation, determines the beer category. The initial fermentation method was wild or spontaneous (still used by Belgian brewers particularly), whereby the grains (sugar supply) are steeped in water and left out in the open for "nature" to do its part. With the development of yeasts in laboratories, it is now packaged in pressed cakes, sprinkles, or in liquid form. For brewing, there are two kinds of yeast, those fermenting at warm temperatures (including Ales, Porters, Stouts, Altbier, Kolsch, and Wheats) and those fermenting at cool or cold temperatures (including Pilsners, Dortmunders, Märzen, Bocks, and American malt liquors).

Warm fermenting makes Ales; cold fermenting makes Lagers. Both can take place in open or closed vessels. Open fermentation does not require covering to ward off contamination and unwanted "stuff" falling in. Closed fermentation is more controlled in a contamination-free vessel that can be monitored for length of fermentation. A secondary fermentation can take place in casks (barrels) in the brewery, or in the bottle/can while it is waiting to be opened and poured.

# Top-Fermented Ales

The following are the top-fermented Ales covered in this chapter:

- Mild Ale
- Bitter Ale
- Pale Ale
- Porter
- Stout
- Milk Stout
- Russian Stout
- Barley Wine
- British Old Ale
- Scotch Ale
- Steam Beer

**Mild Ale** is distinctive to England. It's not widely available in the United States; however, more neighborhood brewpubs have recently been placing Mild Ales on their menu of beers as a satisfying *entry* or *gateway* beer for someone new to Craft brews. I've had Odd Notion brewed by Magic Hat Brewery of Vermont and tasted Goose Island Mild Ale on tap at their Clybourn Brewpub in Chicago. Mild Ales are low in both hops and alcohol, between 2.5 to 4 percent. While described as "thin" in body, they are flavorful and refreshing. Colors range from dark brown to copper, and the taste profiles can include caramel and toffee. Be sure to serve Mild Ales at room temperature.

> **DEFINITIONS**
>
> **Entry** or **gateway** beers are mild flavored, low in alcohol, and "easy to drink" for someone not accustomed to big Craft brews.

**Bitter Ale,** with its glittery copper hue, definitely is the national drink of England. At the far end of Ales from Mild, Bitter Ales are heavily hopped, thus they range from bitter to very bitter. With Ordinary, Special, and Extra Special designations, Bitter Ale has an ABV of between 3 and 7 percent. Redhook Brewery in Seattle, Washington, makes an Extra Special Bitter (ESB), at 5.8 percent ABV. Many local breweries also brew the range or specialize in one of the three. Bitter Ale should be served at room temperature.

**Pale Ale** is a regular at almost every brewpub and brewery in any number of designations. Throughout the United States, Rock Bottom makes Double Barrel Pale Ale; described as having "a slight copper hue, medium body, and light caramel malt sweetness, this Ale is all about the assertive citrus and floral hop finish …." At 7.1 percent ABV, it's a prototype India Pale Ale. Serve at room temperature.

**Porter,** an original British workingman's staple that fell out of fashion, has enjoyed a comeback because of U.S. homebrewers. It's always dark in color, with a mix of malts to give it good body; the malts balance the mix of hops, for a distinctive character within a range of 5 to 7.5 percent ABV. Just about every local brewpub and brewery offers a Porter in a variety of taste profiles, including Smoked Porter. Fuller's London Porter is the epitome example. Serve at room temperature.

**Stout,** like Porter, is surrounded by a lot of local lore from its origins in Ireland. Offshoots cluster around the three classical Stouts. Bitter Stout, identified as simply "Dublin" and spoken of as the successor to Porter, is stronger than Porter; it has more malt for body to balance the larger amount of hops. Dublin Stout is extremely bitter. Guinness Extra is the standard, with 4.0 percent ABV in Ireland and Britain and 5.0 percent for export sales. The complexity of flavors is best released at room temperature, but if you want a summer thirst quencher, serve it chilled.

**Milk Stout,** or Sweet Stout or Cream Stout, contains lactose, a sugar from milk. Lactose is unfermentable by beer yeast. Thus, a Milk Stout is sweet and full-bodied and adds calories to the beer. It is drunk for its added nutrition. Macheson's remains as the only original example of early nineteenth century Milk Stout. Dark in color, it is usually around 5 to 6 percent ABV. Left Hand Brewing Company in Longmont, Colorado is the United States go-to for Milk Stout with the year-round choices of Milk Stout plain or *on nitro*. Left Hand recipes are posted for Milk Stout cake and cupcakes and Milk Stout Barbecue Sauce on Beef Short Ribs. Serve at room temperature.

**DEFINITIONS**

**On nitro,** or nitrogenated beers, have a smoother mouthfeel, a denser and longer-lasting head, and more prominent lacing on the glassware because the bubbles are smaller than in beers that have only oxygen. Nitrogen is infused through mechanical means for beers on draft and in cans. In 2011, Left Hand Brewing Company in Colorado made history by perfecting a way to present nitrogenated Milk Stout in bottles.

**Russian Stout** originated as a British export to the Court of Catherine the Great in Russia and makes for a good barstool story to relate. As with ocean voyage shipments to India for Pale Ale resulting in Imperial Pale, the Stout shipped to Russia gained in hops to survive the journey. Dark in color, Russian Imperial Stouts run around 10 percent ABV. Usually served at room temperature.

**Barley Wines** (sometimes written as *Barleywines*) are closely allied to Russian or Imperial Stout as part of the Big Beers and Strong Ales popular during long cold winters. The modern Barley Wine originated in England around 1870, when Bass brought out its No. 1 Ale. Barley Wine is found in early Greek writings, including the histories by Xenophon and Polybius, who comments that the Phoenicians kept Barley Wine in silver and golden kraters (a large earthen vase). Barley Wines are between 8 to 10 percent ABV and appear red-gold to opaque black in color. This brew is designated Barley Wine because it is as strong as wine but is made from grain, not from fruit. In 1976, Anchor Brewing in San Francisco introduced Barley Wine to the United States with Old Foghorn Barleywine Style Ale. U.S. Barley Wines are more hoppy and thus more bitter than English Barley Wines. Serve at room temperature.

**British Old Ales** have been referred to as "Stock Ales" because they are aged in vats. The color range is very dark brown to almost black, with an ABV of 4 to 12 percent and a wide range of bitterness. Although malts reign, the distinctive qualities of Old Ales are acidic notes along with fruity ones, particularly from raisins and black currants. Strong Old Ales bear similarities to Port Wine. Michigan-based Founders Brewing Company's Curmudgeon Old Ale is a good example of a "malt-forward Ale," at 9.9 percent ABV. Serve at room temperature.

**Scotch Ales** originated in Scotland as strong beers. Asking for a "wee heavy" gets you a "short, strong beer." The descriptions for heavy and light Ales are akin to the English bitter and mild. Scottish-style Ales are prevalent in the United States. Indiana has two high-rated brews: Three Floyds Brewing Company & Brewpub's Robert the Bruce Scottish Ale (6.5 percent ABV) and Sun King

Brewing Company's Wee Mac Brown (5.4 percent ABV). Brooklyn Brewery and Bell's bring out theirs for Christmas. Brooklyn Winter Ale is 6 percent ABV, and Bell's Christmas Ale is 5.4 percent ABV. The tradition is for a long boil in the kettle to caramelize the wort; this produces a deep copper/brown color and a rich mouthfeel with malty flavors and aromas. Hops are floral or herbal and secondary to malt, which sometimes offers a whiff of smokiness. Serve at room temperature.

**BREW WATCH**

Every beer has a story. Scotch Ale's tale revolves around taxes in the nineteenth century. The higher the alcohol level, the higher the taxes so, Scottish brewers named their beers accordingly: 60/– (light), 70/– (heavy), 80/– (export), and 90/– to 160/– for Scotch Ales. The designations remain even though the shilling currency is obsolete.

**Steam Beer** has two diverse connotations, both of which appeared during the nineteenth century. Some breweries that mechanized added *steam* to their names. The longer-lasting designation, however, grew out of necessity during the California Gold Rush years. Miners arriving in the San Francisco Bay area wanted beer. Brewers in the newly created towns and cities learned that ice was a rare commodity. So they invented a different way to brew, and the stories surrounding the activity are as varied as there are tellers. What resulted is a "historic" variety that utilized the nightly cooling breeze that came in from the Bay. To do this, a hybrid style evolved with a top-fermenting Ale technique using available bottom-fermenting Lager yeast. One legend relates that steam floated over the mixture as it was fermenting in huge vats spread across the rooftop of the brewery. Another legend claims that steam hissed out of the casks when they were tapped because the mix of Ale and Lager techniques made a beer with a lively head.

"Modern" Steam Beer has its own legends, the most enduring of which is the saga of deep amber-colored Anchor Steam Beer. The California Gold Rush method of brewing developed into **California Common** and is noted by beer writer Michael Jackson as distinctive to the United States, with both Ale and Lager characteristics. Serve at room temperature or slightly cooler. Interestingly, breweries far from California have been brewing a style of California Common. The BJCP-designated 7B style, utilizing Anchor Steam Beer as the prototype, equally attracts homebrewers.

# Bottom-Fermented Lagers

Lagers ferment at cooler temperatures than Ales. Lagers are further differentiated from Ales by the yeast's ability to ferment all the grain sugars, including the combination of galactose, fructose, and glucose. This makes for a higher alcohol and carbon dioxide level for Lagers. Ales, on the other hand, are sweeter because of the partial breakdown of sugars. Though not "invented" until the middle of the nineteenth century, Lagers quickly spread from their center in Munich, Germany. Today Lager-style beers (with adjuncts instead of the strict German 100 percent barley malt) are the most widespread beer category worldwide.

The following bottom-fermented Lagers are covered in this chapter:

- Munchener

- Schwarzbier

- Vienna (a.k.a. Marzen)

- Pilsner/Pilsener

- Dortmunder

- Bock

- Doppelbock

**BREW WATCH**

In German, *Lager* means "to store." Lagers were stored in cool caves over the summer months to age them, and to preserve them for use instead of upping the hops content, as is done with Ales.

**Munchener** is the original name for the dark-brown beer that is malt centric without being overly sweet. Its aroma hints at chocolate, nuts, caramel, and toffee. In its birth city of Munich, you would ask for a Dunkel, which in German means "dark," to differentiate this Lager from the golden-hued (straw-blonde) Helles. *Helles*, in German, means "light-*colored*" not "lite"—as in beers that have low alcohol and fewer calories because of adjuncts. The Helles Lager originated in Munich and showcased itself through the distinctive clear-glass, vaselike vessel in which it was proudly served. Both dark and blond Munchener brews are moderate in alcohol. Dunkels are served at cellar temperatures (around 50 to 55°F), while Helles are best slightly chilled. ABV is 4.7 to 5.4 percent for Munchener Helles and 4.5 to 5.6 percent for Dunkel.

**Schwarzbier,** a variant from the Dunkel made in the southern Thuringen and northern Franconia regions of Germany, has gained in popularity with the growth of Craft beers. It is usually darker in color than the Dunkel, with a drier palate, slight roasted malt edge, and moderate Noble hop flavor to balance the sweet malt base. It also has a long-lasting, tan-colored head. Serve at cellar temperature. ABV is 4.4 to 5.4 percent.

**Vienna** is the original name for the beer now referred to as Marzen (March beers) in places other than Austria. Marzen and Vienna are also grouped with Oktoberfest (October Festival) beers. Before the invention of refrigeration, brewers in Austria, Germany, and Czechoslovakia figured out that their Lagers tasted better when brewed during colder months. Thus, March was the optimal brewing time for ending brewing, and the designation of "March Beers" indicated those stored in caves and brought out to be served during the summer months. However, some March Beers were indeed more highly hopped to last until October, when brewing started up again. Thus, a festival was held to close out the last of the spring-brewed beers. And so a trio of brews and good drinking fun has come into practice, lasting into the age of refrigeration. Even non–beer-drinkers are aware of every fall's Oktoberfest events, with an emphasis on enjoying the fruits of spring just when winter is closing in. Vienna brews are amber colored, of medium alcohol strength.

Marzen vary in strength, and Oktoberfest brews are strongest in alcohol content. Even the smallest breweries present an Oktoberfest beer for their customers. ABV is 4.5 to 5.5 percent.

**Pilsner/Pilsener** was the breakthrough Lager whose happy fairy-tale ending is similar to that of Rumpelstiltskin, who could weave straw into gold—which happens to be the radiant color of Bohemian Pilsner. The story starts with consumer discontent over seemingly *skunked* Ales in the city of Pilsen (Plzen, then part of Austria–Hungary, now in the Czech Republic). This turn of events was intolerable. Bohemia was already famous for its health-preserving brews, so brewers united to seek help.

**DEFINITIONS**

**Skunked** is a brewing term used to describe contaminated beer that could come about because cleanliness was not strictly observed during brewing, storing, and/or distribution. Skunked beer is as bad as week-old coffee.

In 1840 Bavarian, brewmaster Josef Groll arrived to scope out the situation. Bringing with him skills as a brewer of bottom-fermented Lagers, Groll combined the assets of 1) readily available cold caves and local ingredients with 2) the Lager yeast he brought along. He experimented with making a variation of the popular Munich Bock beer.

Capitalizing on Pilsen's soft well water and aromatic Saaz hops, Groll dismissed using dark-roasted malts and instead developed a light barley malt. When the casks were tapped and the beer was poured, sparkling through the Bohemian cut-glass mug was a clear, straw-colored liquid that dignified itself with a white, long-lasting head. The aroma was befittingly delicate, with whiffs of light malt and spice. The taste sealed the deal.

Completely opposite from their accustomed malt-centric Ales, this new brew's floral note was imparted by Saaz hops, combined with a crisp grain opening mouthfeel and a scant hop bitterness at the fin-ish. The result called for a second round, and maybe a third, at the

Bohemian taverns that had been in business since the 1600s. Word spread, and Pilsner became the worldwide beer of choice, easy to enjoy with a wide array of foods or by itself as a refreshing pick-me-up. It has an ABV of 4.5 to 5.5 percent, with minimal bitterness.

When Pilsner Urquell celebrated its 170th birthday on October 5, 2012, it was an international event signaling that consumers are as savvy now as they were in 1842. And while they are not as aggressive as to dump casks of unacceptable beer into the streets as they did in Pilsen, they are forward enough to show a preference for full-bodied taste in a session beer. German Pilsners are drier than Bohemian Pilsners. Authentic Pilsners should be served chilled, but not below 46°F.

**BREW WATCH**

More consumers are moving away from Pilsner-style knock-off brews from companies that sacrifice quality for bottom line. Replacing 100 percent barley malt with cost-effective filler quantities of rice or corn flakes, these Ersatz Beers deplete flavor and contort the meaning of "light" from color to "lite" for flavor.

**Dortmunder** developed in the coal-mining and steel-manufacturing area around the Ruhr River during the Industrial Revolution. Referred to as the laboring man's answer to the golden Pilsner and the straw-blond Munich Helles, Dortmunder is also described as a blonde beer with a dry palate, at around 5 percent ABV. Dortmund's brewing history is unique. During the thirteenth century, brewers ran the city, but the current number of breweries has dwindled to two, which are fraught with takeovers and changing demographics.

The Dortmunder style has found a year-round counterpart in the state of Ohio with Great Lakes Dortmunder Gold, described as smooth and crisp, balanced between malt and hops, and with a mouthfeel of fresh biscuits or muffins. Shiner Spring Ale Dortmunder is an example of a seasonal by Spoetzl Brewery in Shiner, Texas. Dortmunder has come a long way from the mines and mills of Westphalia. Serve gently chilled.

**Bock** originated as a dark, malt-forward Ale in the Lower Saxony town of Einbeck during the fourteenth century and was adapted by brewers in Munich as a lighter-hued Lager. It has 6 percent or higher ABV.

> **BREW WATCH**
>
> The name of Bock beer is an example of how language can change from its original intent. The citizens of Munich pronounced the city of Einbeck as "ein Bock," which in German translates to "a billy goat." Hence, the inside joke has been to adorn the label with a picture of a goat, since the name has been shortened to Bock.

Bock historically has been the beer consumed by Bavarian monks during times of fasting, providing them with the requisite nutrients to continue their work on a liquid diet. Bock beers continue to be specially brewed for Christmas and Easter, particularly the Lenten season. Maibock, obviously associated with its appearance in May, is a drier, hoppier, more bitter version of traditional Bock. Samuel Adams offers two versions, Winter Lager and Chocolate Bock. Yuengling, the oldest operating brewery in the United States, celebrated its 180th birthday in 2009 by bringing back Yuengling Bock after having discontinued brewing Bock around 1970. Serve a Bock at room temperature or lightly chilled.

**Doppelbock** translates to "double bock" and can have an ABV of between 7.5 and 13 percent. Doppelbock is attributed to Italian Paulaner monks in Bavaria, around the 1620s and 1630s, as a form of "liquid" to drink. Today Dopplebock has more than 200 brand names throughout Germany, each ending in –*ator*: Celebrator, Salvator, Triumphator, and Maximator are examples; Bell's Consecrator is a U.S. example. Their stories are told on the German Beer Institute website. As the name implies, Dopplebocks are big, hearty beers with strong malt throughout and toasty aromas. The color runs deep gold to dark brown. Serve at room temperature or lightly chilled.

# Distinctively Wheat

Wheat beer, though top fermented and thus rightfully part of the Ale category, is in a class by itself. Wheat beer is distinctive because of its preponderance of wheat malt to the usual barley malt of Ales and Lagers, and a specialized yeast capable of imparting aromas and flavors of banana and clove. A spare use of noble hops (Belgium Wit uses spice bundle called gruit) imparts a special taste profile. Wheat beer is known for a thick, white, long-lasting head that creates lovely lace on the glass. Wheat beer is distinctive in both content and context from Ales and Lagers. Furthermore, with a pronounced differentiation among German, Belgian, and American styles, Wheat beer offers variety for an ever-widening palate.

Today Wheat beer is a consumer choice and a delight for brewer adherence to classical brewing methods and for innovation beyond the classic styles. The ratio of wheat and barley used together (and separately) makes the difference in aroma, body, and taste.

**BREW WATCH**

An earthernware crock, the so-called Kassendorf Amphora, found in a Celtic grave near the village of Kassendorf in northern Bavaria, was identified as an earthenware fermentation vessel. It dates beer making in Europe to at least 800 B.C.E. The Kassendorf Amphora contained residues of Black Wheat Ale flavored with oak leaves. This 1934 archeological find has provided the basis for the claim that Wheat beer is the oldest-known brew in Europe, centered in the southern German state of Bavaria.

## Barley vs. Wheat

A bit of upper-class chicanery makes for an intriguing story of barley versus wheat. The story told is that, around the high Middle Ages (somewhere around the thirteenth and fourteenth centuries) rulers began mandating that only barley be used in making beer "for the people," presumably to preserve wheat for making bread, an essential food staple. Two reasons seem to emerge: 1) wheat harvests were generally harder hit by climatic changes, hence a shortage more often happened with wheat than with barley, and 2) it is easier to mill wheat flour for making bread than to mill barley for baking.

However, it was well known that both the ruling class and the monks were allowed to brew the lighter-color, lighter-bodied Wheat beers with a general ratio of 60 percent wheat to 40 percent barley. As for the general population, even though 100 percent malted barley works just fine for brewing, brewers found ways to get around the mandate. The persistence to use wheat in brewing was based on the simple fact that wheat has higher protein content than barley. Hence, beer made with wheat had more food value. When you're subsisting on a liquid diet during a Lenten fast, that protein boost is essential.

But another factor continues to be a source of debate concerning wheat versus barley: Bavaria's *Hefeweizen* is unfiltered, meaning the yeast bits remain with the beer instead of being removed by a filtering process. This is important because the yeast is rich in B-complex vitamins.

 **DEFINITIONS**

*Hefe* in German is yeast, and *weizen* is wheat. Thus, **Hefeweizen** is a Wheat beer with a prominent yeast–wheat presence.

Homebrewer/author Charlie Papazian became an early champion of unfiltered beers. These beers have the benefit of B-complex vitamins, which are essential for the metabolism of fats, carbohydrates, and protein. Papazian's mantra has been, "We need B-complex vitamins to convert the food we eat to useable energy. (The energy or fuel our body synthesizes from food is glucose (blood sugar)." He further posits that B-complex vitamins maintain our energy levels by maintaining the fluid intake in our bodies, which is important for multiple body functions, including brain function.

Nevertheless, the cautionary tale here centers on responsible use. By its very nature, alcohol inhibits the absorption of B-complex vitamins. Current scientific evidence weighing benefits versus liabilities falls on the side of moderation in drinking beer of any kind. Nutritionists say that you can gain B-complex vitamins from foods such as turkey, tuna, whole grains, potatoes, bananas, beans, chili peppers, lentils, and molasses, along with nutritional yeast and brewer's yeast. The best of all possible worlds, according to some, is to drink unfiltered beer while eating foods high in B-complex vitamins.

## From the Wheat Malt Lockout to Today

The Reinheitsgebot of 1516 allegedly was issued in Bavaria to control purity with four ingredients: water, barley malt, hops, and yeast (at the time, yeast was not yet understood and fully controlled, as it is now). There is some discussion about the real intent of this "purity" law—that is, with the edict of barley malt only, wheat was taken out of the reach of brewers for the populace. Only monks and brewers for nobility had access to wheat malt.

This wheat malt "lockout" lasted until 1603, when the Elector of Bavaria contested the Wheat beer shut down. Two hundred years later, the nobility relinquished control of brewing Wheat beer. In the 1800s, anyone could brew beer from either wheat or barley. Why? Fashion changed. The old-style brown beer was gaining popularity over unfiltered wheat. By the 1920s and 1930s, tastes had swung toward filtered beers. They swung back during the 1970s to unfiltered Wheat beers because their fuller flavors and reported health qualities attracted a new generation.

Today Wheat beers are in high demand in Bavaria and worldwide. They are particularly popular in the United States because microbrewers both adhere to style (per the well-known brands) and inventively expand beyond the original models. Traditionally, Wheat beers are associated with summertime, but they have become year-round staples as an easy drinking brew that fits well with a variety of foods, or simply on its own any time of day.

# Wheat Beers

The following Wheat beers are covered in this chapter:

- Bavarian Weisenbier
- Kristalweizen
- Dunkelweizen
- Berliner Weisse
- Leipziger Gose
- Witbier
- Belgian Lambic
- Gueuze
- Mars
- Faro
- Kriek
- Brussels Fruit Lambics

**Southern Germany (Suddeutsche/Bavarian) Weizenbier,** particularly Munich, includes the unfiltered Hefeweizen. Its golden color is made cloudy from wheat proteins and suspended yeast. Aromas and tastes of cloves, banana, apples, citrus, smoke, and sometimes bubble gum come from the specialized yeast and the combination of 60 percent wheat malt and 40 percent light barley malt. Wheat provides a soft, full mouthfeel, and the spare use of noble hops (remember, they're used for aroma) makes for a barely perceptible bittering. ABV is 4.3 to 5.6 percent. Best served between 41°F and 45°F.

**Kristalweizen,** a filtered Hefeweizen, is exactly what it means—"crystal wheat" or crystal clear. Weihenstephaner Kristallweissbier, Paulaner Hefe-Weizen, and DeGroen Weizen (based in Baltimore, Maryland) are considered to be classic brands. ABV is 3 to 5 percent and best served cool, about 46°F to 54°F.

**Dunkelweizen** is a darker (in color) Hefeweizen, with a hint of caramel, toast, or biscuit from the darker roasted malt. Franziskaner Hefe-Weisse Dunkel is a classic brand. Weizenbock is darker still and higher in alcohol, at 7 percent, which intensifies the aroma and flavor; sometimes it feels like a Sherry. Erdinger Pikantus and Schneider Aventinus are classic brands. Alcohol content for German Wheat beers generally is around 5 percent. All are served at cellar temperature.

**Berliner Weisse** (*Weisse* means "white" in German) is nothing like Bavarian Weizenbier. The only similarity is that it's made with wheat, but even here, it's a variation. Bavarian Weizenbier has a 60/40 ratio. Berliner Weisse is closer to 50/50 for wheat and barley, and the yeast is totally different, as are the hops. Berliner Weisse is very tart; its sourness sometimes is mitigated with a touch of raspberry syrup in the pour or heightened with a slice of lemon on the rim of the glass. Low in alcohol, at 3 percent, it's suited to hot summer days, when the beer's inherent flavor (akin to blue cheese) can cut through the humidity. This beer is light and effervescent. It is an acquired taste. The classic brand is Schultheiss Berliner Weisse. Serve at cellar temperature.

**Leipziger Gose,** brewed in Leipzig, Germany, is similar to Berliner Weisse, but is somewhat stronger, at around 4 percent ABV. With the addition of coriander and salt, it is different from German beers. Both Leipziger Gose and Berliner Weisse gain their sourness through the addition of lactic acid bacteria in the fermentation, along with yeast. Serve at 45°F.

**Witbier** (White Beer, Bieère Blanche, or simply Witte) is brewed mainly in the Netherlands and Belgium, where there is documentation of its presence during the Middle Ages. It has been popular for about 200 years. Recurring wars and famines almost wiped out the style, but it rallied until 1955, when the last brewery making Belgian Witte closed. And therein rests another amazing story.

In 1965, Pierre Celis, a milkman in the town of Hoegaarden where Witbier last was brewed, decided to bring back the beer by homebrewing in his father's stable until he could expand into a commercial operation. Sadly, the new location burned and Celis was unable to make his own comeback because he was underinsured and had no other financial backing. Celis sold his Hoegaarden brand to Belgian macrobrewer Interbrew (now Anheuser-Busch InBev), where Hoegarden continues to be brewed.

In 1992, Celis came to Austin, Texas, where he founded Celis Brewery. His Celis White gained a coveted four-star rating from the late Michael Jackson. However, although the beer gained consumer favor, Celis Brewery did not fare well. It was bought out by Miller Brewing Company and closed December 31, 2000. In 2002, the Michigan Brewing Company in Webberville, Michigan, purchased the Celis White brand. The company continued to brew it until 2012, when Michigan Brewing closed. Pierre Celis died at the age of 86 on April 9, 2011, unaware of this turn of events. Yet there is promise of a happy ending after all.

When Michigan Brewing's assets were sold at auction in 2012, the Celis family repurchased the Celis trademark. Christine Celis, Pierre's daughter, has been in the process of developing a new brewery to once again brew Celis White and her father's other recipes. From 1992 to 1998, Celis White gained annual awards at the Great American Beer Festival, and from 2003 to 2010, Celis White continued to be honored worldwide.

Today's Belgian and Dutch White beers descend from the original Medieval Wheat beers. Brewed with a bundle of *gruit*, they contained spices and other plants for flavoring and preserving, but contained no hops because of French regulation during Medieval times. However, currently the gruit is made up of a blend of coriander, orange, bitter orange, and hops, for a slight hop flavor. Belgian and Dutch Wheat beers have a somewhat sour taste because of lactic acid in the brewing process.

**DEFINITIONS**

**Gruit** (or grut) is an herb mixture (usually in a bundle) used for bittering and flavoring beer. It was used before hops became the preferred ingredient. Gruit originally was a combination of herbs including sweet gale, mugwort, yarrow, ground ivy, horehound, and heather. Different herbs were used to gain distinctive flavors.

Witbiers are simultaneously fresh tasting and complex. Like their German cousins, White beers have a second fermentation in the bottle. Some Belgian brewers now also brew fruit-flavored Wheat beers. When Witbier is cold, the wheat proteins and suspended yeast make the beer look hazy and white, hence the name Witbier or Witte which means "white" (as does *blanche*). Classic Belgian Witbiers, in addition to Celis White, include Blanche De Bruxelles and Allagash White. Belgian Wittes should be served at cellar temperature. ABV spans 4.4 percent to 10 percent.

**Belgian Lambic,** though made with wheat and barley, is different from Belgian White beers because Lambic continues to rely on spontaneous fermentation of the wort. For centuries, Brussels Lambic has been exposed to the wild yeasts and bacteria native to the Senne Valley, resulting in a dry, vinous (winelike), cidery flavor with a sour aftertaste. Pure Lambic generally is at least three years old before it is served. Most famous is the Cantillon Brewery and Museum, which continues to make brewing history. ABV is 4.2 percent. Serve at 45°F.

Lambic now is mostly refermented into a variety of derived beers whose origins are associated with a brewery or city or region location and, thereby, are protected under European Union Traditional Specialty Guaranteed (TSG) status. This means you are buying the genuine product when you see the TSG label. While *Lambic* entered English through French, it was actually first Dutch, probably originating in the city of Lembeek in the vicinity of Halle and Brussels.

**Gueuze** is made by mixing together a one-year-old Lambic (young Lambic) and a two- and/or three-year-old Lambic (old Lambic) that have been bottled. The new mixture subsequently undergoes a secondary fermentation, which produces carbon dioxide because the young Lambics are not fully fermented. Gueuze kept in the bottle needs at least a year to referment, but you don't need to open the bottle right away. Gueuze has a dry, cidery, musty, sour taste punctuated by acidic acid and lactic acid and "barnyard" aromas. Today brewers might add sugar to the mixture to sweeten the brew and make it less mouth puckering.

Gueuze can be kept for 10 to 20 years; open one whenever you like, and it will have the same taste and aroma. Because Gueuze is highly carbonated, it is sometimes referred to as "Brussels Champagne" and is served in large (25 oz.) or smaller (12.7 oz.) champagne bottles. There is no definitive etymology for the origin of the name Gueuze. (Do not confuse Brussels Gueuze with Leipziger Gose, described previously.) Serve at room temperature or slightly chilled. ABV is 5 to 6 percent.

**Mars** is a weaker Lambic that no longer is produced. Although it has totally gone out of favor, one never knows when tastes will change. Served at cellar temperature, with ABV around 6 percent.

**Faro,** on the other hand, continues to be produced as an inexpensive, light, and sweet everyday beer. Originally, it was a low-alcohol combination of two different styles—a year-aged Lambic and Meertsbier (a freshly brewed beer that is lighter than Lambic)—sweetened just before serving with the addition of brown sugar or caramel or molasses and sometimes herbs. Modern Faro, no longer characterized as a cheap or light beer, is a bottled Lambic (not Meertsbier) with the addition of brown sugar that is pasteurized to prevent refermentation in the bottle. Lindemans Faro (from Vlezenbeek, Belgium) is a modern classic example. It is served at room temperature or slightly chilled. ABV is 8 percent.

**Kriek** (Dutch meaning "cherries") is Lambic refermented for a year with the addition of sour Morello cherries (pits included). Kriek has a dry, sour, cherry taste, but without sweetness because no sugar is added. ABV is 4 percent. Serve at about 60°F.

**Brussels Fruit Lambics** are distinctive, with the addition of black currant (cassis), peach (pêche), raspberry (framboise), or strawberry (aardbei) preferably as the whole fresh fruit. Other traditional fruit additions can be apple (pomme), apricot (abricotier), banana (banane), blueberry (bleuet), cloudberry (plaquebière), lemon (citron), pineapple (ananas), and plum (prunier). Fruit Lambics are bottled with secondary fermentation and should not be confused with a different line of Belgian fruit beers not made from a Lambic base. These nontraditional fruit beers basically are riding the popularity coattails of Fruit Lambics and do not have the same quality ingredients; therefore, they lack the distinctive taste profile of a traditional Fruit Lambic. ABV is 5 to 6.5 percent. Serve at 45 to 55°F.

**American Wheat** is the American Craft brewers' "spin" on traditional Wheat beers from the German and Belgian traditions. Refer to the section "Widening Wheat's Horizons," in Chapter 7, for more information.

## The Least You Need to Know

- A beer's style refers to a specific set of ingredients and balance between these ingredients. Three classical styles of beer are Ale, Lager, and Wheat.

- Ales are made with barley malt and are top fermented. Lagers are brewed with barley malt and are bottom fermented. Wheat beers are brewed with barley malt and some wheat, and are top fermented.

- Wheat beers are unique because of the brewing process, their taste profile, and the distinctive thick, long-lasting head that leaves a lovely lace pattern on the glass as you drink.

- It's not enough to know the statistics of the beer's ingredients. Getting the full story about a brew helps you appreciate what's in your hand and what's entering your body, making you a part of the lore.

# The American Craft Brewing Industry

## In This Chapter

- Americanizing Classical Amber Ales, Brown Ales, Porters, and Stouts
- Taking Lagers back to their flavorful roots
- Expanding the American palate with Wheat beers and Fruit beers

The motivated homebrewer became the backbone of the American Craft brewing industry. With an understanding of the European traditional and classical styles, homebrewers utilized ingredients available where they were living and coupled adaptation and innovation with their skills for replicating recipes both handed down and sought out.

In this chapter, we traverse how the American style of brewing emerged and developed from acceptable, to accepted, to an advancing style of brews as homebrewers opened breweries and brewpubs and slowly grew the Craft industry.

# The Return of Ales

Military personnel returning home from posts in Europe desiring to maintain the range of foods and beers they had been introduced to become another mitigating force for beer with character. Jack McAuliffe did more than wish—in 1976, he opened New Albion Brewing Company to produce British-style Ales. New Albion became the clarion call to return to our original roots with Ales.

Then came Fritz Maytag, at Anchor Brewing, offering a new look at Ales to mark the bicentennial of the 1775 midnight ride of Paul Revere and the start of the American War of Independence. Beer writer Michael Jackson described Anchor Liberty Ale as "the first modern American Ale with the prominent use of Cascade hops and a change to the recipe using all malt instead of the expected malt and sugar." Maytag visited breweries in London, learned the traditional styles and brewing methods, and came home to create an original brew—and perhaps another revolution of sorts. By 1983, Anchor Liberty Ale had found a steady audience and became a regular in the Anchor lineup of brews. The ready supply of local hops with distinctive character certainly played a part in the development of hop-centric American Ales.

In 1982, Scotland-born Bert Grant opened Yakima Brewing & Malting Company. Also known as Grant's Brewery Pub, this became the prototype upon which succeeding brewpubs were developed. Grant produced a Pale Ale, followed by an Amber, IPA, and Scottish Ale. But the first to specifically name its beer American Pale Ale was Sierra Nevada Brewing. In 1981, the brewery called it "a delightful interpretation of a classic style … with generous quantities of premium Cascade hops [to] give the Pale Ale its fragrant bouquet."

**BREW WATCH**

Another impetus for change away from Lagers produced to look and taste alike, no matter who bottled or canned them, was U.S. citizens traveling to Europe. These travelers came home with a broadened view of bread beyond sliced white, cheese beyond American brick, and, yes, beer beyond "lite."

Full-flavored Ales became the microbrewers' primary innovation to offer the public a choice of real beer in addition to (or, they hoped, in place of) the plethora of same-Lager-fits-all products from different companies. While originally based on the diversity of English, Scottish, Irish, and German Ales, American Craft brewers individually and collectively developed a bolder, more aggressive taste spectrum to forge an American style using American-grown barley malted in the United States and American-grown hops.

Though each brewer has a personal recipe, you can generally expect American Ales to be maltier and hoppier than the originals from Europe. Be assured that many Craft brewers can and do brew well-made Ales according to British styles. Brooklyn Brewing provides one of the shining examples of true British character. But as the Brewers Association (B.A.) points out, given freedom (and, most often, necessity) to veer from the classic recipes, U.S. Craft brewers utilize traditional Ale yeast with different ratios of malt to hops. The spin comes from a preference for U.S.-grown Alpha (bittering) hops, particularly Cascade.

The B.A. description provides a general guide for what to expect from an American Ale, particularly "a brisk bitterness and aroma of American hops," as opposed to the "toasted caramel sweetness" you expect with a British Ale. As a result, the aroma is different—citrusy and fruity for American, instead of the British grassy. And if the British brewers thought their India Pale Ales were bold, they do indeed "pale" alongside big American Imperial IPAs and Double IPAs. It's sort of a game of two-upsmanship—if one handful of hops is good, two must be better.

But it hasn't been just brassier Pale Ales for the sake of affecting an attitude in a vacuum. A number of social and cultural changes were going on simultaneously, all propelled by aspects of connecting back into our own American history and reaching out into the wider world.

# The Americanizing of Amber Ales

If American Pale Ales set the course for a style to satisfy the hop-heads, it is with Amber Ales that Craft brewers intended to break loose of the stranglehold of the macrobrewing Lite Lager industry by inventing another uniquely American style from the traditional Irish Amber. American Craft Amber Ale's moderate strength (with a spectrum of taste from first sip to final swallow) showed the American public they could opt for a moderate-alcohol, slightly hop-forward brew with layers of flavor emanating from a caramel maltiness. This was, and still is, a gateway beer to Craft brews.

Brewers/owners John and Gregg Hall built a reputation on Honkers Ale at Goose Island Beer Company in Chicago. With a meshing of old British and new American qualities, this everyday Pale Amber beer is as much at home with barbecue as it is with fish and chips. Again, as new brewpubs and breweries opened, American Amber became a standard.

American Red Ale was next to take a step away from its traditional Red Ale ancestors, with a "burnt sugar quality" as a balance to "discreet or enthusiastic" amounts of hops. Described as "easy to drink, hard to define," American Reds ask us to think about the qualities of toasty malt, with a light fruitiness and a hop presence that can range from subtle to strong. While *Irish* and *Red Ale* seem synonymous with St. Patrick's Day, Irish Reds are fun for any day. With a history tracing Irish Red first appearing in the town of Kilkenny in 1710, it makes sense that Boston should heartily embrace the industry leader Samuel Adams Irish Red.

**TASTING TIP**

It's equally right that South Bend, Indiana, should be the home city for the Four Horsemen Brewing Company, so named to honor the Fighting Irish of Notre Dame University. Their Irish-style Red Ale, distinctly American, with a hoppy bite to close out the opening sweet, nutty, toasty mouthfeel, earned a bronze medal in 2012 at the U.S. Beer Championship. Samuel Adams Red took the gold.

If Red Amber doesn't win you over into Craft, perhaps American Brown Ale is the style to do so. Starting at a mere 4 percent ABV, and using American malts and hops, it provides rich caramel notes rising to toasty, lightly roasty aromas—especially enticing in winter. Brown Ale originated in England but around the 1800s it died out when brewers preferred the less-expensive pale malt over the more costly brown malts. Browns in England thereafter have had an up-and-down history. American homebrewers are credited with reviving and building a consumer base for the steady resurgence of Browns with a robust malt character that balances out stronger hops. Aroma can range from fresh to citrusy.

In his must-read, definitive book *The Brewmaster's Table*, Garret Oliver describes how Brown Ale became distinctly American at Brooklyn Brewing. Bill Moeller, who preceded Oliver as brewmaster at Brooklyn, "introduced Brooklyn Brown Ale as a holiday beer in the winter of 1989–1990. It was powerfully flavored and dry-hopped, like nothing anyone had tasted before. It became so popular that Brooklyn Brewery decided to retain it as the second beer in the lineup." When other brewers followed Moeller's lead, "a new style of brown was on the move."

The power of one brewer to affect change doesn't allude to strength as much as it does to inventiveness. Craft brewers love to tinker, which, of course, opens the debate to matters of consistency. Yet when tinkering leads to something particularly special, the recipe is saved and shared. Likewise, consumers let the brewer know when it's time to let things be and just make another batch.

# Accessing Porters and Stouts

American Porter and American Stout are perhaps more like their British antecedents in strength than are the currently produced British Porters and Stouts. Both are described as having plenty of roastiness and sometimes a tinge of caramel, always balanced by American hops.

Garrett Oliver writes in his *The Brewmaster's Table*, "You would be hard-pressed to find an American Craft brewer who isn't in love with stout." I agree. It is my personal favorite, and when in doubt, I'll opt for a Stout, having made the acquaintance in Britain at an early age. And well-made American Stouts "with a depth of roast and hop character" are the top of the line. Oliver's description veers into poetry: "Citrusy American hop aromas may leap out of the glass, blended with coffee and cocoa aromas." To him, the high bitterness "is married to an espresso-like bite from the heavy use of roasted grains."

Basically, good American Stouts are beers that keep on giving, even after the glass has been drained, because of the abundance of ingredients. Each ingredient gives its all in appearance, aroma, and flavor. Anchor Brewing Company first brewed Porter in 1974 and set the standard for East Coast, Midwest, and Southwest brewers whose market-reach is almost nationwide. Here are some great examples:

> Magic Hat Brewing Company's sweet Heart of Darkness "inky-black" Oatmeal Stout is marked by a smooth, round palate on top of bittersweet chocolate. Available in the winter, it was reintroduced in Winter 2012 after a hiatus.

> Bell's Kalamazoo Stout, offers a blend of dark chocolate and coffee flavors with just a hint of brewer's licorice. Its description as an American Stout stems from a significant hop presence against the roast malt body.

> Brooklyn Black Chocolate Stout's inky black body topped by a tan head has alluring layers of coffee and fruity, winy, dark chocolate aromas. Bitterness is muted by upfront malts sharing chocolate and coffee flavors for a softly rounded, satisfying mouthfeel. It's a meal unto itself, and extremely satisfying.

> Sierra Nevada and Rogue Brewing each offer a Porter and a Stout. Sierra Nevada's Porter emphasizes hops upfront against a dark roast. Rogue Brewing Company's Mocha Porter addresses every serious chocolate lover with the plentiful taste of bittersweet and a light cream finish.

All in all, distinctly American Stouts and Porters—with their lean toward chocolate maltiness, creamy mouthfeel, and bright tinge of hops—remain the harbingers of beer's essentiality.

# IPA the American Way

To bring us back to brassy and in-your-face, we have American brewers' version of a jarringly bitter IPA—Imperial or Double IPA. These distinctly high alcohol recipes call for hops high on resiny aroma. As a group, American brewers tend to up the IPA ante for higher alcohol and bitterness, utilizing Cascade hops in particular to take the traditional India Pale to places never dreamed of a century ago.

Classic American Imperial/Double IPAs include Dogfish Head 90 Minute IPA, Bell's Hopslam, Russian River Brewing Pliny the Elder, Stone Brewing Ruination IPA, and Victory Brewing Hop Wallop. The names say it all.

# Beyond Bold with Barleywine

American Barleywine made a bold appearance nationwide during the 1980s and 1990s, and continues to grow into the twenty-first century. Definitely a winter seasonal, it's not a wine at all. It's the biggest beer—extremely strong and intense, and coyly hiding its alcohol level.

Though based on the original English Barleywine, it's a very serious-minded beer with a tendency to be maliciously playful. Its huge alcohol level engages in a game of hide-and-seek around a range of fruity, sweet-to-bittersweet flavors that keep you sipping and looking for more fun. The serving size necessarily is limited because a range between 8 and 15 percent ABV has impact. However, well-made American Barleywines have a significant malt character to hold up the hops; this malt backbone distinguishes American Barleywines from American Imperial or Double IPAs. Most Barleywines are intended to be cellared and aged, to be served years later.

> **TASTING TIP**
>
> Lafayette Brewing Company (LBC) in Lafayette, Indiana, makes Barleywines, including the amazing Big Boris. They don't get on the national review blogs because you have to go to Lafayette to taste them. And that brings us once again to the importance of walking in, sitting down, and enjoying a meal with beer, because many local breweries actually are brewpubs. While buying bottled and canned beer that is nationally and regionally distributed is a good thing, supporting local brewpubs and breweries is essential for the continuing vitality of the Craft industry. Nationally, you'll find Sierra Nevada Bigfoot, Victory Old Horizontal, Brooklyn Monster Ale, Avery Hog Heaven Barleywine, and Bell's ThirdCoast Old Ale, among a hundred other Barleywine listings. Every winter, every brewer goes for big.

# Widening Wheat's Horizons in America

On the other side of the solstice, when summer comes around, our late-nineteenth and early-twentieth-century Germanic heritage comes to the fore with American versions of Wheat beer. These Wheats are distinctive because the American style veers from the traditional yeast strains indigenous to German and Belgian Wheats. In place of the German clove and banana flavors and the Belgian spiciness, American Wheats (with their own house yeasts) are tilted toward the wheat tartness and hop bitterness, for a lighter, brighter palate.

Usually rated as "uncomplicated," American Wheats brewed as a summer seasonal are refreshing and excellent for lighter fare. It is believed Portland, Oregon–based Widmer Brothers pioneered the style in 1985, appropriating the name Hefeweizen, but not delivering on the expectation of a true German Hefe. Nevertheless, it is uniquely American and got others started brewing Wheat beers.

**TASTING TIP**

A distinctly American take on traditional beers is to brew it when you want to drink it—as opposed to only during specific seasons—and not to worry about sticking to style. So why not make a cross between a Wheat and an IPA? Magic Hat, in South Burlington, Vermont, offers a winter seasonal that does just that.

If other brewers taste a beer and decide it's worthy of replication, as is the way with Craft brewers, they'll contact the head brewer and chat about the brew and then develop their own recipe. After they brew it, if it's what they intended, then they'll offer it to the public. Replication increases the buzz beyond the initial "new brew." After some time, a different style fits comfortably into the regular lineup. Patrons of the Craft grow to expect the unexpected.

# American Fruit and Vegetable Beers

American fruit and vegetable beers follow brewing's longest-running tradition of adding fruits to flavor, aid fermentation, and preserve a brew. The epicenter of fruit beers resides in Belgium, and the best of American fruit beers follow this tradition.

New Glarus Brewing Company in Wisconsin, Pyramid Brewing in Washington, and Upland Brewing Company in Indiana have gained dedicated local, regional, and national reputations with their Lambics (see the section "Lambics in America"). They go beyond fermenting with the traditional cherries, raspberries, blackberries, and peaches, as have the Belgian brewers in recent times. Using distinctive bottles, these companies have achieved close to cult status with fall releases.

Most American fruit beers are built upon an American-style Wheat beer and a variety of locally sourced fruits. These fruits are introduced into the fermenting or conditioning stages and are annually anticipated by a public who appreciates the neighborhood and small regional brewers who go out of their way to deliver fruit beers.

**BREW WATCH**

While the fruit crisis of 2012 did not reach proportions of the 2009–2010 worldwide hops crisis or the 2011 lean U.S. barley harvest, many small breweries scrambled after the poor fall 2012 harvest to obtain fresh fruits for their small batch seasonals.

In 2009, Allagash Brewing Company gained attention with a Saison made with sweet potatoes and black peppercorns. This version of Allagash's annual "tribute series beers" was a bronze-medal winner in the 2010 World Beer Cup and was reviewed as having "high complexity with great balance," but it was brewed only once and currently is retired. Nevertheless, this merger of traditional American south and traditional Saison has caught the fancy of homebrewers. Several have entered sweet potato beers into competitions.

# American Lagers

Well-made American Lagers indeed have a place at our tables, in our backyards, and at the bar. They remain clear, pale-straw to medium-yellow in color with a thin, frothy head. The Standard American Lager presents a crisp and dry flavor, sometimes offering a corn-like sweetness. The Premium American Lager is bolder than either the Lite American Lager (from macrobrewers) or even the Standard American Lager. Premium has an ABV range from 4.6 to 6 percent as opposed to Lite's 2.8 to 4.2 percent and Standard's 4.2 to 5.3 percent.

American Lagers retain the requisite refreshing and thirst-quenching character, though the Premiums tend to be more filling due to the increase of malt in order to balance the increase in hops. While Premium import beers have fewer adjuncts such as rice and flaked corn, the distinguishing factor for Craft American Lagers is an all-malt recipe. However, newly made American Lagers (replicating early American Lagers) require some corn to provide the expected sweetness.

In 1985, Jim Koch was the first to brew a full-flavored Lager, with the Vienna-style Samuel Adams Boston Lager. Brooklyn Brewing followed in 1987 with Brooklyn Lager, which became its flagship beer. A marriage of German and American ingredients created a distinctive, versatile style—American Amber Lager, with a touch of sweetness and snappy bitterness, to make it an all-around beer suitable for any cuisine.

# Lambics in America

While conventional Ales and Lagers are fermented from cultivated strains of brewer's yeasts, Lambics developed before anyone understood that fermentation was caused by microorganisms—in fact, even before anyone knew what a microorganism was. Brewers simply left the sweet wort open to the air, often in the attics of their barns, and wild yeast and microflora landed in it and did their magic, eating sugar and producing alcohol. The result of this spontaneous fermentation is a beer like no other: dry and quenching, with a slightly sour aftertaste.

Lambics pose a conundrum for American Craft brewers who strive to be highly sanitized and keep wild yeast out of their brewing operations. However, around 2006, Allagash Brewing Company in Maine (followed soon after by Russian River Brewing in California and Jolly Pumpkin Artisan Ales in Michigan) made news by actively inviting wild yeast into a specially secured spot in their breweries. This was taking them, and us, back to ancient methods of brewing before we understood the source of fermentation.

You usually have to travel to the breweries to get a taste because it's hard to find bottles in every corner of the United States. Allagah Spontaneous, Russian River Resurgum, and Jolly Pumpkin Lambicus Dexterius began to challenge us with tart sourness. The result is a puckering first sip that doesn't abate but does get more familiar as your mouth adjusts to a very different set of awakenings—sort of like sipping a rainbow and tasting each color sometimes separately and sometimes swirled together.

The challenge for small Craft brewers is that the process of brewing requires aging the first Lambic brew for a number of years. This means having to wait for two things: 1) to discover whether the final result is indeed what was desired (since wild yeasts are uncontrollable) and 2) a delayed return on investment.

Nevertheless, Lambic is produced in two distinct styles: with fruit or without fruit. You're quite likely to find a brewery nearby sourcing locally grown fruits for a Fruit Lambic with a dominant tart cherry, raspberry, or Muscat grape aroma and flavor. Fruit Lambic is a moderately big beer with an ABV between 5 to 7 percent, while Straight Lambic runs between 5 to 6.2 percent ABV.

Lambic dries with age. Its complex, sour/acidic mouthfeel emanates from the relationship between the malt and the wild yeast strains. Hops are utilized more as preservatives than for bittering. What sets American Lambics apart from classic Belgian Lambics is the use of American grown grains and hops and the reality that wild yeasts vary from place to place.

**TASTING TIP**

Upland Brewing Company, in Indiana, follows traditional Lambic-brewing practices. A turbid mash of boiled, unmalted wheat is conducted before mashing in with a balance of Pilsner and Pale Malts. Unlike the common infusion mashing technique used to produce most Lagers and Ales, this method allows wild yeast, *brettanomyces,* to feed on a more diverse sugar and dextrin (low-weight carbohydrates) content.

After a long kettle boil, the mixture is hopped with three-year-old Hallertauer that has lost most of its alpha acid content, creating a beer with minimal bitterness that also retains the preservative qualities of the hops.

Batches of Upland Lambic are fermented with a combination of yeast and various other microorganisms selected to create a strong, pleasant tartness aged in white oak casks for over a year while the sour and acidic qualities slowly develop. Then in the case of the Lambics, Upland brewers add fruit, which prompts a second fermentation and adds another layer to the already complex flavors and aromas of the beer. To the dantalion, they add a blend of spices instead of fruit, which complements the sourness developed during fermentation. After aging for several more months in the barrel, the brewers bottle-condition the beer for several weeks to achieve a fresh, zesty carbonation.

## The Least You Need to Know

- American Craft brewers begin with a base of classical styles and, utilizing the ingredients on hand, build upon tradition to grow the industry with integrity, quality, and consistency.

- The return to Classic Ales countered a century of one-kind-fits-all Lagers. While many brewers retain the Classic recipes, others interjected the bold use of American-grown hops for a bigger beer profile.

- The Ale revolution that began in 1976 was followed by the Lagers revolution with American brewers taking the crisp, clean tasting brew back to a variety of taste profiles.

- A third and fourth movement took American brewers to adapting Classic Wheat beers and Classic Fruit beers to expand American beers even further.

# The Art of Beer Tasting

With the history and process of brewing happily in mind, you're well prepared to join the ongoing journey of discovery since that very first brew so long ago. Tasting Craft beer unleashes powers of observation, smell, taste, and feel you didn't know you had. To fully experience the variety of styles, each with its own layers of complexity, you learn to take your time through a series of steps that build your abilities to detect subtleties and gain a vocabulary to talk about what you are experiencing.

The brewer's passion, craft, and artistry transform the four main ingredients—water, grain, hops, and yeast—into a bouquet of liquid pleasure. And now you are becoming part of the tradition. But remember, taste is very personal. You don't have to like everything you taste. Nevertheless, you may want to stretch your buds, and Part 3 guides you to do that.

# Experiencing Your Beer's Taste

Chapter

# 8

## In This Chapter

- Finding places to taste great beer
- Following six important steps in beer tasting
- Discerning the flavors of malt and hops
- Building your beer vocabulary and tasting notebook

You've learned that beer is comprised of two major categories: Ales and Lagers. In addition, you know that there are multiple styles and substyles under each category and that brewers strive to make the best possible beer within a style. Now you learn how to really taste beer so that you experience what the brewer intended.

# Where to Go to Taste

Craft beer tasting is a social event. Aside from the obvious brewpub or production brewery tasting room, here are some places you should check out to meet up with people who enjoy Craft beer as much as you:

- Taprooms or bars that serve beer on draft (also spelled *drought*) regularly invite the public to a tapping of a new Craft brew by a local or regional brewer.

- Homebrew supply stores often sponsor meetings where brewers exchange information and share homebrews. Visitors are usually welcome.

- Liquor stores that carry Craft beers may have tasting events for bottled and canned Craft beer hosted by people who are knowledgeable about beer.

- Communities with an established Craft beer culture usually have tasting events. Check local newspapers and/or on activity websites.

- Craft beer festivals often attract a wide range of brewers, offering you a way to taste brews not ordinarily found where you live.

- National groups such as Girls Pint Out and Barleys Angels create tasting parties (check out their website for a chapter near you).

If you're just getting interested and don't know anyone who can help you connect with a beer-tasting event or group, the best place to start is your local liquor store. Check the shelves. If the beer selection includes choices from smaller breweries, ask a clerk whether the store has tasting events. If the answer is no, ask if it's possible to get one started if you promise to attend. If that's not possible, ask if you can leave your name and contact information for the owner to connect you with a customer or two who's already familiar with the store's stock. Inquire whether the store also carries homebrew sup-plies. Homebrewers are definitely assets in your pursuit to become a knowledgeable Craft beer patron. Find a way to meet them and get into their circles.

> **TASTING TIP**
>
> Because brewing is chemistry, each new batch of beer might taste slightly different from the original recipe. Consistency is an everyday challenge. Sometimes patrons who regularly visit a brewpub claim they can detect variations in their favorite beer. Sometimes brewers smile at their claims.

If none of the foregoing exists in your place of residence, short of moving permanently, consider a visit to another community with Craft beer amenities. Ask the clerk for any and all recommendations of places to go to for someone just diving into Craft to meet other likeminded people. Ask for the stock items closest to a Craft beer, make the purchase, and, once home, use the rest of this chapter to help you prepare your tasting. Invite a friend or family member aged 21 or over to join you on a journey of beer discovery. Remember, making connections and sharing knowledge is the Craft beer way.

## Proper Temperature Is Critical

Craft beer should not be too cold. The serving temperature rule of thumb is as follows:

45°F–50°F for Pale Lagers

50°F–55°F for Amber and Dark Lagers and Pale Ales

55°F–60°F for Dark Ales and Stouts

Craft beers share their complexities as they warm. Never serve or drink Craft beer in a frosted glass. The ultracold inhibits the beer's aromas and flavors from opening up. In scientific terms, condensa-tion occurs, dilutes the beer, and robs you of its value.

# The Six Steps to a Proper Tasting

Proper beer tasting involves six key steps. If you follow them correctly, you'll be able to experience a beer in all its glory, just as the brewmaster intended when developing the recipe.

## 1. The Opening Act

Some people might think that you don't need to worry about opening a beer properly, but how you open the can or bottle can greatly affect the end result. When you open a bottle, avoid shaking it. Hold the bottle firmly on a flat surface with one hand; with the other hand, flip off the top with a beer bottle opener. When you open a can, avoid shaking it. Hold the can firmly on a flat surface with one hand; with the other hand, pull the tab.

## 2. The Art of the Proper Pour

Artisan beer is enjoyed best drunk from a glass. Even ballpark vendors pour your bottle or can Craft choice into a plastic cup. Why? Drinking from the bottle or can robs you of the pleasures of sight and smell—you miss seeing the hue and catching the aromas, two important companions to fully enjoying the taste of a Craft beer.

When you're served in a public place, someone else is pouring the beer. Observe how they pour and what the results are. Although pouring is not an exact science, you get the best results by using glassware designed to showcase the special qualities of a particular style (refer to Chapter 9). It is also generally agreed that the best way to garner all the good beer qualities is to tilt the glass at a 45° angle, to allow a little of the liquid to slide down the side, and then straighten the glass and pour down the middle.

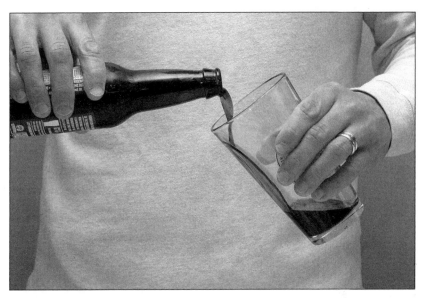

*Tilt the glass at a 45° angle, to allow a little of the liquid to slide down the side.*

Opinions vary on how fast to pour. Some servers say you should never hurry pouring, especially for unfiltered Wheat beers. You should place the bottle or can straight down into the glass, and when there's about three fingers of beer left in the bottle or can, you should take it out, turn it upright, swirl to loosen the yeast bits from the bottom, and then pour all of the beer into the glass.

On the other hand, some servers pour quickly, to "rouse the carbonation" and get a thick head. And some experts advocate "sloshing" the beer into the glass, to open it up. In time, you will find the pouring style that fits you. The point is to allow the beer to meet and greet you cordially and for you to return the compliment.

**TASTING TIP**

Opinions vary on pouring the yeast bits that are part of unfiltered Wheat beers into the drinking glass. If you don't like "chewy beer," leave the bits in the bottle or can.

## 3. Befriending a Brew by Sight

Appearance affects expectations of what's to come. Visually examining a beer tells you it's fresh and ready to be drunk:

- **Look at the head.** Is it thin or dense? If dense, is it "rocky" or smooth? Some beers are supposed to be bubbly, with a head of peaks and valleys as bubbles pop, but generally, a well-made beer should "keep its head" for at least a minute and leave a lacy rim as it recedes.

- **Look at the body of the beer.** What is the body color? Hold the glass to the light to get the fullness of the color. The color ranges from green sunlight to opaque black across the 23 styles identified by the Brewers Association, Beer Judge Certification Program, and the American Homebrewers Association. Color is determined by how long the grains are in the kiln. Light malts make light beers, and dark malts make dark beers. Is the body properly clear or cloudy, according to style? Note that some unfiltered beers have bits floating around.

**TASTING TIP**

A Hefeweizen should have a dense head, and the body should be cloudy because it is unfiltered. A Pilsner's head should be pure white and its body like sunlight. Stout and Porter heads are light to medium brown over an opaque body.

Each beer style is brewed to present a unique appearance, and brewers take pride in immediately determining whether their brew meets the guidelines.

# 4. The Aura of Aroma

Sniffing your beer makes it clear you're smart about the art. But sniff quickly—beer scent is volatile and disappears fast. Immediately after viewing, sniff at least three times.

The rule of thumb is that light-hued beers have a strong hops bouquet that is unique to each style. Hops aroma gives off piney, resinous, herbal, floral, and spicy notes (sometimes even bitter and antiseptic).

Aromas from the grains and malt are basically fresh and earthy and can be described as nutty, malty, sweet, and/or grainy. Grains are kilned at different lengths of time to impart a particular aroma. Malt is more prominent in darker-hued beers as roasted chocolate and coffee. Malts are more apparent in Porters and Stouts.

**TASTING TIP**

Lagers have fewer taste layers than Ales. Ale complexities continue to grow as the beer warms.

Ale aromas are more complex than Lagers because their Ale yeast spiciness or fruitiness is hard to pin down.

If a beer has an odor other than these, it has a problem and should be discarded. Skunkiness might come from being stored too long or having had too much exposure to light. Other off-aromas might come across as sulphury, buttery, fishy, oily, or chloriney.

# 5. Taste Buds at Work

Our tongues are home to about 10,000 taste buds, made up of 50 to 100 receptors. Each has a specific job to detect five known primary taste sensations: sweet (like sugar), sour (like lemon), salty (well, salt), bitter (stale, cold coffee), and umami (MSG). Our taste buds are also able to discern numerous combinations of tastes made up from a mix-and-match of these five.

For about a hundred years, school textbooks have promoted a "tongue map" showing specific locations on the tongue where we are supposed to taste sweet, sour, salty, and bitter (the original tongue taste artist didn't know about Asian cuisine, so umami is absent). A lot of school kids ended up failing the proscribed taste zone test because we spoke up and said, "Hey, I taste sweet, sour, and bitter on the tip of my tongue, not just salty." Finally, we misfits are reprieved. A research report in the August 2010 issue of *Journal of Cell Biology* debunks this erroneously rigid tongue map and expands our understanding of the differences between "taste" and "flavor sensations."

Your taste buds are a combination of nature and nurture, so come prepared to succumb to or overcome preferences you've been nurturing for the past 21 years (or more). "You know what you like, and you like what you know" is a truism that you take with you into beer tasting.

## 6. Sip and Savor

Now take a dainty sip—yes, dainty—not a hefty swig. This is where your personal taste reigns over Beer Judge Certification Program (BJCP) guidelines.

Here's what to pay attention to:

- **Mouthfeel.** This is how heavy the body of the beer feels in your mouth—is it light, medium, or full?

- **Flavor.** This is how the hop bitterness and malt sweetness mate together in your mouth—are they loving and compatible, contentious, or nondescript?

- **Finish.** This is what you're left with after you swallow—is it just over and done with, or is there an enjoyable, lingering memory?

Notice your first sensation as beer passes your lips, touches your tongue, and enters and fills your mouth. Can you separate the malt from the hops tastes? For example, it's common for specific malts to render Dry Stouts silky, Scotch Ales thick and chewy, Berliner Weisses thin and fizzy, while Wheat beers as a whole are expected to be rich, creamy, and refreshing.

Fully tasting flavor requires being able to separate what is imparted from malts, hops, and yeast. Generally, a beer gets its sweetness from malts, its bitterness from hops, and its multiple other tastes from yeasts.

One of the best ways to learn how to discern malt flavors in a brewed beer is to smell and taste grains before they get into the brew. Brewers are always chomping on ingredients singly and in varying combinations. It's their way of figuring out ahead of time how a brew will taste if they write up a menu with $X$ percent of this and $Y$ percent of that in combination with $Z$ amount of water. A homebrew supply shop is a good place to visit and graze the bins, chewing a pinch and making careful note of what you are tasting.

# Flavor: Maltiness vs. Hoppiness

Brewers use a variety of malts that have been roasted or toasted, from light, to dark, to darkest. Used alone or in combinations in the grist bill (amount of grain in the recipe), these different malts impart their flavors in accordance with the percent of their presence in relation to each other in the recipe. Beers made with more toasted malts impart flavors such as toast or bread crust, perhaps seem nutty, or taste like a graham cracker.

Using dark roasted grains as the major ingredient creates flavors close to chocolate and coffee and could give the beer a degree of bitterness. The lighter roasted crystal and caramel malts give their beers a range of flavors, including caramel, toffee, molasses, and sometimes an upfront taste of burnt sugar. Some dark malts give a beer fruit flavors, such as plums or prunes. Rauch beers get their distinctive smoky flavor from deliberately smoked grains. Generally, a beer gets its sweetness from malts.

> **TASTING TIP**
>
> Think of malt taste as you would varieties of malted milkshakes, malt vinegar, and malted milk ball candies. These have a distinctive flavor profile that you can describe because you are familiar with them.

"Malt-forward" beers include such differing styles as Vienna Lagers and English Barleywines, along with Scottish Ales and German Doppelbocks.

American brews are distinctive from others as "hops forward," leading off with distinctive American Pale Ales, India Pale Ales, and Double IPAs. American Pilsners are perhaps the model of "hops forward," with the Saaz noble hops overriding pale malt.

Discerning a balance toward hops might seem easier than figuring out malts, but which hops? We know that the gentle bitterness referred to as "bite" comes from bittering hops. Aromatic hops are more prominent as a "grassy" nose.

## Know Your Hops

The number of hops varieties is staggering. Twenty countries worldwide are currently growing 216 kinds of hops, with research underway for even more.

### Number of Hops Varieties by Country

| | | |
|---|---|---|
| Australia 11 | France 4 | Slovenia 3 |
| Austria 1 | Germany 24 | South Africa 4 |
| Belgium 3 | Japan 8 | Sweden 1 |
| Canada 1 | New Zealand 13 | Switzerland 2 |
| China 8 | Poland 5 | The Ukraine 16 |
| Czech Republic 6 | Russia 1 | United States 51 |
| England 48 | Serbia 6 | |

About the best an ordinary person can do is get to know the distinctive qualities of a reasonable number and bow in admiration to brewers who constantly are being challenged to learn about new products.

**BREW WATCH**

The hops harvest failures in Europe and some parts of the United States in 2008 and 2009 forced many brewers to investigate hops growing in far-flung locations. As a result, some Craft breweries restructured recipes and renamed beers.

Nevertheless, it is quite instructive to take some time to find freshly harvested hops and rub the flowers between your fingers to discern distinctive scents. Tasting freshly picked hops is not a smart option. Many breweries and brewpubs grow small amounts of hops for local use in a seasonal fall brew. They usually put out a sprig for educational purposes.

## Find the Balance

Some people prefer a beer's balance toward malt, and some want hops to override (they're known as "hopheads"). Brewers as a whole work to achieve balance, adding more malt as a strong backbone for a massive injection of hops. Conversely, they want even the maltiest brew to have some zing. So look for the balance in the beer's overall properties of acidity, bitterness, dryness, esteriness, fruitiness, hoppiness, and richness. Fuller beers have more malted barley in relation to water.

Yeast and water equally affect taste and balance. Yeast is what makes a beer smooth on one hand or sharply winelike on the other. Water can be soft, hard, alkaline, or acidic. Any one of these is an asset for certain styles, and brewers can choose to brand their product according to the available local water source. Water also can be treated, to mimic any required attribute for a style. But just as your personal choice dictates a preference for more malt or more hops, the kind of water you usually drink can affect your choice of a brew.

> **BREW WATCH**
>
> A multidisciplinary group of professors at Butler University in Indianapolis undertook an interesting water experiment in 2010. In the experiment, titled "Turning Water into Beer and Other Small Miracles," four faculty homebrewers "brewed two batches of a Cream Ale using the same recipe but different water sources to highlight the role water plays in the brewing process."
>
> A blind tasting was held at a public event on December 3, with 21+-year-olds tasting each batch. Guests were asked whether they regularly drink bottled water or tap water before they chose which of the two brews they liked best. The tally showed that people who drink bottled water preferred the beer made with treated water. The people who drink tap water preferred the beer made with tap water.

## Register the Aftertaste

Even though it's taken a lot of reading to get here, it takes only about two minutes to allow a brew to extend its levels of complexity in your mouth. It takes another minute for you to register the aftertaste after you have swallowed a time—or two or three. Be assured that you want to register a pleasant aftertaste. It's a beer's way of being gone but not forgotten, like the scent of a spring shower lingering after the rainbow has faded.

So take the minute to think about aftertaste. If there's excessive alcohol or carbonation, you're left a bit unsettled. You might want to give it another try, to determine whether the finish will improve with warming. If, on the other hand, the beer is clean and pleasant going down your gullet and spreading across your shoulders and into your body, you want to take another sip and move past analysis to simply enjoy the rest of the glass.

# Talking the Taste

Be sure to read the brewer's description, and try to match what to expect with what you actually feel as the beer fills your mouth. This helps you build a vocabulary of descriptive terms that are universal to beer tasting. Maybe the brewer's "refreshing" claim falls short in your mouthfeel. How can you articulate what you do feel? Is it more heavy than refreshing? Or more thin and watery than refreshing?

Another way to build your beer vocabulary is to read beer reviews on websites and in magazine and newspaper columns. Some reviewers are straightforward; some wax poetic. When a reviewer compares and contrasts several brands in a particular style, if at all possible, with a copy of the review in hand, find those beers and taste them at your leisure. Compare what you're tasting to the reviewer's description.

Now that you know how to describe what you're experiencing, take some notes!

# Start Your Tasting Notebook

As you broaden your palate and work your way across the Craft-brewing universe, a tasting notebook is a handy way to keep track of past tasting experiences and will be useful to refer to down the road. It helps you compare similar styles and record how subtle characteristics can affect your tasting experiences. Following is a template you can use for your journal.

Tasting Date: _____

Tasting Place: _____

Brand Name: _____

Style: _____

❏ Draft   ❏ Bottle   ❏ Can

❏ Served in Special Glassware   ❏ Generic Glassware

Appearance: _____

_____

Aroma: _____

_____

First Sip Flavor: _____

_____

Mouthfeel: _____

_____

Swallow Feel: _____

_____

Aftertaste: _____

_____

Overall Impression: _____

_____

_____

## The Least You Need to Know

- Places to taste include brewpubs, brewery tasting rooms, bars, pubs and taverns, and liquor stores.

- All your senses are involved with enjoying the complexities of Craft-brewed beers, including sight, smell, taste, touch, and hearing (when you converse about qualities).

- Artisan beer has its particular vocabulary for discerning its qualities. You can acquire vocabulary from various sources.

- Keeping a journal builds a handy reference tool and is simply fun for recalling when you first found what's now your favorite brews.

# Taking Taste to the Next Level

## In This Chapter

- Learning to taste like a Cicerone
- Recognizing undesirable odors and tastes
- Using the Meilgaard Wheel to build your taste vocabulary
- Discerning the substyles of Pilsner

Now that you've learned how to taste beer, you're ready to gain experience in discerning the nuances between styles and between brands brewed in a particular style. As you gain experience by tasting a greater variety of beers, you find the differences and similarities and acquire the vocabulary to articulate what you are observing, smelling, tasting, and feeling.

It's a slow process that gives you pleasure over time. The best part is that there's always a new brew to taste, old favorites to go back to, and people around who value your opinion. There's no right or wrong answer when you're at a tapping or tasting event and someone you know or haven't even met asks, "So what do you think?"

# Tasting (and Thinking) Like a Cicerone

A Certified Cicerone in the Craft beer industry is similar to a Certified Sommelier in the Craft wine industry. The first level of the Cicerone program is to earn status as a Certified Beer Server. This requires intimate knowledge of beer styles, off-styles, and off-flavors; proper glassware for each style and proper glassware washing; and knowledge of federal and state laws surrounding beer. The highest level is Master Cicerone, which requires extensive study to pass the exam to exemplify broad Craft beer knowledge. The titles Certified Cicerone and Master Cicerone are protected certification trademarks of the Chicago-based Cicerone Certification Program. The program seeks to improve beer quality by certifying the knowledge and tasting skills of those who sell and serve beer.

Cari Crowe is a Certified Cicerone. Her job is to train servers and bartenders in restaurants, taverns, bars, and Craft beer tasting rooms in how to serve beer properly and how to use this expertise with customers. Cari explains, "I'm responsible for making beer an exciting experience on all levels. It's daunting and humbling at the same time to spend your time captivating people for their personal enjoyment. We want to captivate, not bore people. I like tasting to be a poetic, visceral experience."

Our book utilizes Cari's special tasting method to teach you how to "see, swirl, smell, sip, and swallow" while tasting beer. Some debate surrounds which should come first, the visual or the aromatic; decide for yourself which suits you best.

## See

When we "see" the beer through a clear glass, we're talking about observing the beer's color, effervescence, and head. It's also smart to make sure there are no improperly floating objects in your beer. Of course, with an unfiltered beer, like a Wit or Wheat, many of us want the chewy bits to be part of the drinking experience.

**Color.** Hold the tasting glass up to the light. You want to enjoy the beer's distinctive color because we are visually attracted to hue as part of an overall culinary experience. In addition, take note of the visual range of lite Lagers to robust, dark Porters. Note that this is also the way servers line up a tasting fleet—lightest to darkest.

*The color*

Brewers determine the beer's color density according to the SRM scale (Standard Reference Method). Each beer style has its range of hue/tint within a spectrum articulated as follows:

Straw

Yellow

Gold

Amber

Deep amber/light copper

Deep copper/light brown

Brown

Dark brown

Very dark brown

Black, opaque

**Effervescence.** Along with enjoying the color, a beer with bubbles delivers delight for the same reasons we enjoy a sparkling wine or Champagne. It's simply fun to observe the effervescence of a sparkling Pilsner and it feels somewhat elegant to be holding up a pitch-black Stout.

**Head.** Paying attention to the head adds to the pleasure. While a thin-head beer doesn't deter us from drinking, for some reason, a 2-inch foam seems mighty attractive. And it's the foam that delivers the protein, truly making beer a food and beverage in one.

## Swirl and Smell

Swirl and sniff/smell are essential to obtain clues to remembering the style of beer you have in hand. It might take a time or two to accomplish the right amount of swirl in a full glass, but it's worth the practice to learn how to release the beer's aroma. As long as the pour or head isn't at the very top of the glass, you should easily be able to swirl the glass a few times.

*The swirl*

Tilt the glass so that the beer is close to the edge, and put your nose to the lip of the glass. Slowly breathe in through your nose for a couple seconds, as the aroma is released. Swirl a time or two before you sip, then swirl intermittently as you sip to help release all the fine characteristics of the beer. Swirling tends to release aromas so swirling and sniffing/smelling are simultaneous actions. Some styles such as Belgians automatically invite swirling and sniffing/smelling because enjoying the aroma and the layers of flavors are essential to the enjoyment.

*The smell*

Here are some examples of typical aromatic descriptions for common beer styles (as a rule of thumb, the darker the color, the fuller the aroma):

> *Lite and Standard American Lagers* aren't supposed to offer much aroma. This kicks up a notch with *Premium American Lagers* for a low to medium-low malt whiff, perhaps a bit grainy or sweet like corn.

> *Munich Helles* and *Dortmunder Export* aromas enable you to experience the significance of their place of origin. For the Munich, the clean Pils malt dominates as grainy-sweet and is balanced by a low, spicy noble hop layer; the Dortmunder might go further with an initial scent of sulfur from the water and/or yeast, but then it gratefully fades.

> *Pilsners* tend to be described as "clean." We want a clean character in Lager beers.

> *German Wheat* and *Rye beers* up the aroma ante with desirable yeast phenols imparting cloves or esters of banana or other fruits.

When sniffing the beer's aroma, pay attention to whether what you're discerning matches the beer's style. Hopefully, such an error would have been caught before a brew got to you, but sometimes a new homebrewer cooks up an uh-oh batch that's off-style. Most times we laugh it off and drink it anyway.

## Sip

The first sip awakens your mouth to flavor. Every style has its particular profile. Once tasted, you don't forget an authentic Vienna Lager, with its upfront soft, complex malt elegance coupled with direct hop bitterness. The specialness comes with the medium-light to medium body and creamy mouthfeel, giving way to a somewhat dry, crisp finish to keep the rich German malt backbone from becoming overly sweet.

As you become more adept at discerning flavor and mouthfeel you'll discover the nuances among American, European, and Mexican versions. American brewers tend to go for a stronger, drier, more bitter recipe, while European brewers lean more toward sweetness. The Mexican versions that originally were authentic now are brewed with less Vienna or Munich barley malt and more corn, for a thinner brew.

*The sip*

As the sip moves into your mouth for a "savor," with an authentic Vienna Lager, you will notice moderate carbonation with the creaminess. It's a smooth, crisp feel, not at all biting.

## Swallow

Swallowing arouses a full-body sensation as the liquid moves from mouth to the larynx and into the esophagus and "down the hatch," so to speak. Your mouth lets you know right away if you're liking what you're tasting. The actual swallowing arouses a different set of sensors—is the liquid too hot, too cold, just right? Is it smooth or cloying going down? Beer further has a quality that "touches" the shoulders. Hard to explain, it is nevertheless felt. A warming beer in the winter, such as a Barley Wine, will tingle warm with the swallow. A cooling, crisp beer in the summer such as a Pale Ale, with the swallow will cause the body to cool down. Your body reacts to what you swallow and lets you know if it's pleasant or not. That's why seasonal beers are popular.

*The swallow*

With the swallow, a Vienna Lager might give you a slight alcohol warming feel down your throat and around your shoulders. The crisp finish cleans your palate and readies you for another sip. How you describe your overall impression is personal, yet the expectation is that you will discern a certain elegant maltiness matched by a touch of hop bitterness. You will want to remember the experience of a Vienna Lager in comparison with the more popular Oktoberfest/ Marzen beers. Boulevard Brewing Company's Bobs 47 is a commercial example that the Beer Judge Certificate Program suggests for a Vienna-style Lager, yet it's marketed as an Oktoberfest. So the crossover and closeness of these two European Amber Lagers challenges us to pay attention to nuances of taste and marketing.

## The Lacing

Between sips, swallows, and savors, take time to notice the effects of the head etching into lace. Lace is foam that sticks to the glass. Beers with a thick, foamy, long-lasting head are the best beer lace makers. Belgian beers are particularly noted for their lace effect. Wheat beers equally provide a pretty foam picture inside your glass. Both the Vienna Lager and the Oktoberfest are noted for their off-white heads that tend to maintain a presence through many sips.

Proteins in the beer contribute to the head and thus the lace. There are two other factors that will encourage lace to form: a clean glass and the shape of the glass. A dirty glass or a glass that has soap residue will inhibit lace formation. And some glass shapes nurture the foamy head and thus lacing. (You'll learn more about glassware in Chapter 10.)

*The lacing*

# The Meilgaard Wheel

The Meilgaard Wheel is a way of "being on the same page" with brewers, beer judges, and beer writers. It gives us a universal vocabulary for determining the quality, reliability, and consistency of a particular brew within a designated style profile. Refer to the Tear Card at the front of the book that displays the Meilgaard Wheel. Going around the wheel as judges drink a beer, they determine its good (and not-so-good) qualities in a way that allows them to compare a personal evaluation with someone else's. Judges are equally concerned with the cleanliness of glassware and the correct pour into the glass.

Judges, servers of beer, beer writers, and quality control scientists in breweries use the Meilgaard Wheel to determine the safety and consistency to style of every brew they taste. The value of the wheel to you is to acquire skills in ferreting out what is unwanted in a beer while developing a palate to savor the delicious aspects of a well-made beer.

Scientists have identified more than 1,000 flavors in beer, yet even an experienced beer taster can pick out only fewer than 100. The average person has a range of half of that. The goal is to keep expanding the ability to taste different flavors. Interestingly, the more discernment you acquire with the beer, the greater your capacity to enjoy the nuances of all other foods. Beer is food, thus drinking beer with the intention of widening and broadening your palate is a direct way to enhance your enjoyment of all foods—and life in general.

Meilgaard's Wheel is divided into 14 categories that are broken down into 44 flavors. These have become the standardized way that beer tasters correlate word-to-flavor descriptions. These are particularly important to beer judges, who are not only rating a beer, but also helping a brewer to improve. For every off-flavor, there is a known cause or cluster of causes, so the judge can guide a brewer to review the recipe and procedure and determine what needs to be corrected in either or both.

To become adept at building a beer-tasting vocabulary, thoroughly familiarize yourself with the wheel and its descriptions of *odor* and *taste*. Start with the *odor* side of the wheel because aroma is our initial sensory contact.

## Undesirable Odors

Sniff quickly to determine that the beer has none of these unwanted smells that signal the beer is spoiled, termed as "off-flavors":

- **Oxidized, stale, musty:** You don't want beer smelling moldy, leathery, papery, catty, or stale.

- **Sulphury:** These off-flavors include unpleasant yeastiness that's meaty, cooked vegetables (particularly corn), sulfitic like a struck match, rubbery, rotten, and egg.

- **Soapy, fatty, diacetyl, oily, rancid:** You don't want your beer to smell rancid, like mineral or vegetable oil, or with smells of butterscotch, fatty acid, soap, or cheese.

- **Phenolic:** This refers to smelling or tasting like plastic, adhesive strips, or a medicinal (think cough syrup or mouthwash).

- **Caramelized, roasted, and cereal:** These feel husky/grainy or dry, as the result of poor balance between hops and malt. Some beers with flaked corn are supposed to have a cereal feel.

- **Resinous, nutty, green, grassy:** These relate to mustiness.

- **Chlorophenol:** This refers to odors of plastic, vinyl, or iodine.

- **Aromatic, fragrant, fruity, floral:** These refer to being perfumy. Aceteldehyde refers to smelling or tasting like fresh-cut green apples, rotten apples, or cut pumpkin. Fruit Lambics are supposed to impart the aroma of the dominant fruit in the beer.

> **TASTING TIP**
>
> Two aspects you need to sort out per proper style are smoke and clove-like spiciness. Smoked beer is supposed to smell and taste smokey. Belgian Ales and some Wheat beers are supposed to have spicy aromas.

Do not drink a beer that smells like chlorine or solvents such as lacquer, paint, or paint thinner. Spoiled beer is different from skunked beer. The particular "skunky" odor results from overexposure to light of any kind, indoors or outdoors.

## Undesirable Tastes

With the first sip, determine whether the beer style is off-flavor because the fullness is off-balance. Watery beer means there's not enough malt compared with water. Be aware that some beer styles are thinner in fullness than others—if you prefer a fuller beer, you need to stick with those styles. Also determine whether the mouth-feel falls into these categories:

- **Warming:** Alcoholic spicy is not desired. The warming effect of a Barley Wine is a pleasant feeling.

- **Carbonation:** Too gassy or flat.

- **Powdery:** Dry, like overdone toast, or dry as a result of grains being steeped too long.

- **Astringent:** Mouth puckering, tart, vinegary.

- **Metallic:** Tinny or rusty.

- **Mouthcoating:** Too creamy; blots out other flavors.

- **Alkaline:** Tastes like detergent.

## Proper Balance

Determine the balance among the four basic tastes that comes through the proper balance of the four ingredients—salt, sweet, sour, and bitter:

- **Salty:** You do not want salty beer.

- **Syrupy sweet:** Overly sweet and cloyingly sweet indicate poor balance between hops and malt.

- **Sour:** Similar to sour milk; acrid.

- **Acetic:** Vinegary.

- **Acidic:** Refers to sourness. Do not feel compelled to drink a beer with an off-flavor that is not within the parameters of the style. Acidic taste is to be expected with Sour beers; if it's acidic and not a Sour beer, do not drink it. Estery is to be expected with Belgian Ales and German Wheat beer, but generally beers are not supposed to taste fruity.

- **Bitter:** Bittering in beer emanates from the brand of hops. The Craft is to balance the sweet malt with the right amount of hops so as to impart a clean, crisp mouthfeel for Pale Ales, a bit of hops kick for Imperial brews, a creamy sweetness for Wheat beers.

Learn what to expect from each style and judge its quality accordingly.

# Putting the Meilgaard Wheel to the "Taste" Test

The best way to learn to use the Meilgaard Wheel, and thus build discernment and vocabulary, is to drink a beer while you go around the wheel. We'll walk you through a Pilsner substyle example, and after that, you can gather with friends to help each other gain facility in discerning specific qualities of each.

As you taste and chat, use the vocabulary of brewers:

- **Mouthfeel:** A pleasing warmth and a pleasing balance between hops and malt; crisp, clean; aggressive or mild or in between; hop-centric, malt-centric but overpowering on either end; possibly multiple layers or simple. Can you name the flavors, or are they just out of reach?

- **Body:** The sensation of being thin, light, medium, or full in your mouth; watery or creamy; robust and full bodied or subtle. Can you describe the feel?

Discerning the substyles of Pilsner helps you learn that some qualities not desired in other styles are perfectly acceptable for this style. In beer tasting, it is important not to fall into a "black/white," "either/or" attitude. Follow along to learn the nuances of the three substyles of a Pilsner in accordance to what is generally expected.

> **TASTING TIP**
>
> The distinctive aroma and flavor profile of some beers comes directly from individual yeast strains. For Hefeweizen, the clove and banana flavor comes from the yeast. Abbey Ale yeasts provide the estery profile and the slightly spicy character. Each Pilsner substyle (German, Bohemian, Classic American) has its particular yeast strain, hence three very distinctive aroma and flavor aspects.

Begin with properly pouring a beer into a glass free of soap scum or greasy residue of any kind. When in doubt about total cleanliness, swish the glass with a splash of beer, swirl the beer to cover the entire interior surface, and then spill out the beer. This cleans your glass for a good beer experience, ensuring the proper head, scent, and display of the beer's body.

## German Pilsner

If you can't find a local brewery or brewpub that offers a German Pilsner, try one of the commercial examples suggested by the Beer Judge Certification Program (BJCP) for learning to be a beer judge.

From Germany:

- Bitburger
- Holsten Pils
- Konig Pilsner
- Spaten Pils
- Trumer Pils
- Warsteiner

From the United States:

- Brooklyn Pilsner

- Left Hand Polestar Pilsner

- Old Dominion Tupper's Hop Pocket Pils

- Victory Prima Pils

If none of these are available, ask your local bottle shop for help in finding a German Pilsner.

This is what you are looking for with German Pilsner (Pils).

Aroma:

- Malt that smells like Graham crackers.

- The special flowery/spicy scent of noble hops, such as Hallertauer, Tettnanger, and Spalt.

- Clean.

- No fruity ester.

- No diacetyl. However, the malt might give off a cooked vegetable whiff at the start, and sometimes the water or yeast gives off a whiff of sulfur. This should not linger.

Flavor:

- Leans a bit to malt at first, but should move to hop-bitterness for the finish and the aftertaste.

- Medium to light body.

- Medium to light carbonation.

- Refreshing.

- Crisp.

**BREW WATCH**

Take time to absorb the expected qualities and to become fluent in talking about what you are experiencing. Determine whether a style is one you truly enjoy, can pass on, or really don't find worth drinking. As you move through the rest of this chapter use this wrap-up exercise for each of the following exercises: What am I experiencing? Do I like this beer? What don't I like? If yes, what do I like? If no, what don't I like? Is there one brand I like better than any of the others? Why? Build a compare and contrast vocabulary between brands in each style.

## Bohemian Pilsner

The following are some commercial alternatives, if you can't find anything locally:

- Czech Rebel
- Czechvar (Budweiser Budvar in Europe)
- Pilsner Urquell
- Dock Street Bohemian Pilsner
- Gambrinus Pilsner
- Zaty Bazant Olden Pheasant
- Sam Adams Noble Pils
- Harpoon Bohemian Pilsner

This is what you are looking for with Bohemian Pilsner.

Aroma:

- Malt that is richly layered in aromas.
- Saaz hops that have a floral bouquet.
- Clean.
- No fruity esters.

Flavor:

- Starts with rich malt.

- Follows with short-lived hops bitterness overtaken by hops spiciness.

- Balance between hops and malt at the end.

- Clean.

- No fruity esters.

- Refreshing.

- Crisp.

- Fuller body than German Pilsner.

- Lower carbonation than German Pilsner.

Now that you have allowed your sensory capacity to wrap itself around Classic European Pilsners, you can move on to American Pilsners. As you experience, take time to note cultural differences along with noting the general expectations for the Pilsner style.

## Classic American Pilsner (CAP)

Visit your local brewpub and your bottle shop for the local brands. Classic American Pilsners are uniquely brewed to ingredients that were available in the nineteenth-century United States. As of the moment, there are no national selling brands. Local brewers who are into recreating Classic American Pilsners must do a lot of research to replace a variety of hops and yeasts that no longer exist.

Craftsman Brewing Company, in California, offers 1903 Lager, a Pre-Prohibition Pale Lager brewed with a lot of corn. Upland Brewing Company in Indiana has recreated the Pre-Prohibition Champagne Velvet as CV, with a profile close to the original yet pleasing to twenty-first century consumers.

Aroma:

- Some grainy, cornlike or sweet maltiness.

- Medium to high hop aroma, using clusters, continental noble hops, or modern noble crosses such as Crystal, Liberty, and Ultra.

- Clean.

- No fruitiness.

- No diacetyl.

- Some DMS (dimethyl sulphides) as in cooked corn, but not overpowering.

Flavor:

- Medium to high maltiness.

- Grainy, cornlike sweetness from up to 30 percent corn to 70 percent barley (usually flaked maize, most recently Briess has developed a corn malt for Classic American Pilsner brewing).

- High hops to balance corn sweetness, but should not be harsh. If rice is used, the flavor is crisper than with corn, which is sweeter.

- Creamy-rich mouthfeel.

- Medium to high carbonation.

- Medium body.

- Refreshing.

- Should not have any coarseness because of water with high mineral content.

- No fruitiness.

- No diacetyl (butterscotch, butter, or slickness in mouthfeel).

## Summing Up Your Taste

When you have finished tasting each of the substyles, note your overall impression of each. How do they compare with each other in difference and sameness? What qualities make them a Pilsner, despite having unique national/cultural qualities? Which do you most enjoy drinking? Why?

The Meilgaard Wheel is a tool to develop a vocabulary when chatting about beer. But begin to develop your own descriptive phrases as well. Make tasting Craft beer personal to the flavors and aromas you already have collected in your sensory bank. The dividends pay off in feeling what you see, smell, and taste. Flavor is a composite of all we perceive.

## The Least You Need to Know

- A Certified Cicerone has intimate knowledge of beer styles, off-styles, and off-flavors, along with proper glassware for each style and knowledge of federal and state laws surrounding beer.

- Brewers determine the beer's color density according to the SRM scale (Standard Reference Method). Color is determined by how long the grains are in the kiln. Light malts make light beers; dark malts make dark beers.

- The Meilgaard Wheel utilizes a vocabulary for determining the quality, reliability, and consistency of a particular brew within a designated style profile.

- The best way to learn to use the Meilgaard Wheel, and thus build discernment and vocabulary, is to drink a beer while you go around the wheel.

# The Right Glass for the Right Beer

## In This Chapter

- Discerning the shape of beer glassware for specific styles
- Getting familiar with the nomenclature of glassware particular to Germany
- Washing beer glassware

Sometimes the most heated conversations concerning beer can be about glassware, whether it is too particular or too casual. So just how much, you might ask, does the shape of glassware matter when you're going for the ultimate essence of hue, aroma, and taste of an Artisan beer? Even the experts have agreed to disagree. Use this chapter as an aid to gather information, taste-test, and choose what most suits your preferences.

While using glassware to match the style is the best of all possible worlds, some experts claim a brandy snifter is a good all-around substitute because its shape allows every style to showcase its specialties. Other experts say the easily stored ordinary pint glass is fine if you are careful to pour slowly, allowing the beer to aerate and prepare itself to be drunk. Interestingly, the touch of specific glassware brings you into the story of that brew. It's the context in which the beer resides, sharing its past with you in the moment of savoring it.

# The Significance of Shape

The earliest depiction (around 3200 b.c.e.) of a beer vessel appears on a cylinder seal from ancient Mesopotamia. Two people seated on chairs opposite each other are drinking from a knee-high clay pot through straws. This clues us in on how the straws filtered out possible unwanted items in the liquid.

**BREW WATCH**

Though the shape of the Mesopotamian clay pot hasn't received much analysis, perhaps someday someone will look into its similarity to present-day Scotch Ale thistle-shaped glassware.

Special glass shapes have been developed over centuries to impart the best qualities of a specific brew. Some are named for their shape, some for the beer served. Some reflect national traditions or a brewery's particular brand to showcase the brew's unique qualities. Some are generated by folk artists and have become our favorite vessels. On a recent trip touring Belgian breweries, I carefully brought home glassware that I enjoy because of both the good memories and its ability to showcase Belgian brands that I'm able to purchase in the United States.

# The Glassware Guide

For general purposes, here's a rundown of glassware for each style. For your own purposes, you might want to start with matching glassware to one or two styles you particularly enjoy drinking and then add glassware as you grow more favorites. Generally, you will utilize this chapter for what to expect when beer is poured by knowledgeable servers at public establishments.

**TASTING TIP**

Never serve Craft beer in a frosted glass. It ruins the good work of the brewer by inhibiting the flavors. Why? Beer at near-frozen temperature numbs the taste buds. This results in bland-tasting beer instead of releasing a variety of tastes in layers of complexity. Aroma is equally affected. In a freezer, frost picks up flavors of other stored foods. Thus, the frost on the glass smells like the freezer and tastes like anything else in there.

## The American Shaker Pint

The American shaker pint, with its wide mouth sloping to a narrower base, is most associated with beer in the United States. It's used because it's easy to stack, wash, and dry, and it's less costly than the specially shaped glassware developed to capture the unique nuances of multiflavored, multiaroma beers. While the wide mouth makes for easy drinking, aromas and heads tend to get lost quickly. Thus, the shaker pint is best for beers with a thinner head and a not-so-vibrant aroma.

*American shaker pint*

Use for: American Amber Ale, American Red Ale, American Wheat Ale, American Amber Lager, American India Pale Ale, Belgian-style Golden Ale, Dortmunder Lager, Rye Ale, India Pale Ale (IPA).

## Pint Glasses

The pint glass, with a slight flair to the mouth that then indents toward a slight bulge before slimming slightly toward the foot, particularly captures and showcases a frothy head and the aroma of malt-centric brews.

*Pint glass 1*

Use for: English Porters and Stouts, American Brown Porter, Barrel-aged American Stout, American Ambers, American Reds, American Hybrids, Black Lager, Cherry Stout, Chocolate Stout, Dry Stout (English and English style), Fruit Beer, Scottish Ale, Smoked Porter, Strong Black Ale, Sweet Stout, English Brown Ale.

Another pint glass shape features a wide mouth and a body that, halfway down, subtly tapers toward the foot. It is lauded as accenting the aromas of earthy British hops, particularly East Kent Goldings. This shape also allows for more head to show and more lace to cling.

*Pint glass 2*

Use for: English Pale Ales, American Pale Ales where hops dominate, Amber Lager, American Rye Ale, American Dark Wheat Ale, Extra-special Bitter.

A tumbler-shaped pint glass is straight down from mouth to foot and also is used with foamy brews. In Germany, Rauchbier (smoked beer) is usually served in a tumbler, called a Willibecher, or shortened to Becher, which means a cup.

*Tumbler pint*

Use for: Light Hybrids, Cream Ales, Blond Ales, Kolsch, American Wheat Beers, Smoked Beers, Fruit Beers (although I have a preference for tulip glassware for fruit beers, to capture both the hue and the essence of fruitiness).

## Handled Glass or Stoneware Mug (German Seidel or Stein)

The handled glass mug, also known as the German seidel and the stoneware stein, is the other vessel most associated with beer. Originally designed to best serve German-style beers, the mug has become the emblem of brewpubs, with their popular mug clubs. Many brewpubs have developed relationships with ceramic artists and glassblowers to create individualized mugs for members, and they proudly display the creations in cabinets or specially designed shelves in the brewpub.

In Germany, especially in Bavaria, the mug is deliberately heavy, for a couple reasons. First, it can withstand use in beer halls with clinking toasts. Second, the handle keeps your hand off the glass—this particular beer style is preferred colder than most other beers.

The stoneware stein with a lid came into use during the Black Plague, when it was necessary to keep flies out of the stein because beer was the only safe beverage to drink at that time. Flies in the beer would infest it, rendering it unsafe. The covered stein continues to be used especially in outdoor settings for the very same reason—to keep flies out of the beer.

*Handled glass mug*

Use for: Oktoberfest, Marzen, Vienna, Munich Dunkel, Schwarzbier. (But don't give this short list to a mug club member who expects to be drinking any beer on tap from his or her special mug. It's a point of pride to rack up pints in your very own mug.)

## Pilsner Glasses

No definitive Pilsner glass exists. The tall glass can be straight sided from a wide mouth, slimming down to a slender foot that can be fluted or not. Or the sides can be softly curved, from a wide mouth to about two-thirds down, where the curve dents in and then flares out to its foot.

Some people like a stemmed glass for a Pilsner beer. Stemmed glasses are called *pokals*. You will find Pilsner pokals in various sizes and shapes, such as a squat, full-bodied tulip on a tall stem or a tall, slender, yet unopened tulip on a short stem. Pilsner (Pils) glassware in Germany is called a pokal because it has a stem. In the United States, a Pilsner glass is in the shape of an inverted cone on a short pedestal.

 **DEFINITIONS**

**Pokal** is German for a tall drinking cup.

*Pilsner glass*

The classic Pilsner flute is not the same as the champagne flute, despite a seeming similarity. Nevertheless, for the sake of staying within budget, if you already have a cache of champagne flutes, use them. Essentially, there's a bit of poetry going on here. The Pilsner beer's sparkling color seems svelte in the tall, slender shape, and the "pillowy" head is served by the conical shape at the top. The aromas are guided through the narrowness of the glass as you lift to sip.

*Classic Pilsner flute*

Use for: Bohemian Pilsner, German Pilsner (of course), Scotch Ale, Berliner Weisse, Kolsch, Dusseldorfer Altbier, Cream Ale, California Common Beer, Dortmunder Export.

The stockier 12-ounce pokal serves malty beers the best by presenting sweet aromas and keeping a head of foam. (Though it's similar to the Pilsner flute, note the slight differences. Yes, Craft beers are that sensitive.)

*Pokal*

Use for: Scotch Ale, Weisenbock, Heller Bock (also known as Maibock), Bock.

## Weizen Glass

The Weissbier "vase" (Weizen glass) has a tall, sloping shape with a wide mouth crafted specially to serve Wheat beer's aromas and foamy head. From a distance, these appear to be the same as Pilsner glasses, but upon comparing the two, you will notice the Wheat glass mouth curves inward and generally proceeds toward the indentation and foot in a softer curve. Weissbier (weizenbier) glassware is a large-sized (usually 0.5 L) inverted cone shape without a pedestal. It holds a long drink of beer.

Use for: Bavarian Hefeweisse, Munich Dunkel, Dunkelweizen, Hefeweizen, Kristlweizen, Weizenbock, Gose, American Dark Wheat Ale, American Pale Wheat Ale.

*Weizen glass*

## Stange

The *stange's* tall, slender cylinder shape best showcases delicate beers when you want to capture and hold nuances of both hops and malt in balance. The narrower the glass, the more able it is to concentrate a beer's highly volatile aspects, which you want to be able to appreciate for a longer time.

**DEFINITIONS**

**Stange** in German means "stick." Although it's similar to a Pilsner glass, a stange is taller and more slender.

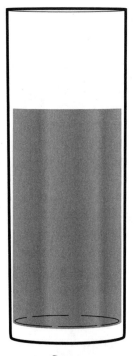

*Stange*

Use for: Rye Beer, Lambics (fruit and unblended), Czech Pilsener, Atlbier, Bock, Gose, Gueuze, Kolch, Rauchbir (smoked beer).

## Stemmed Abbey Goblet

The stemmed abbey goblet is perhaps the most elegant, designed by breweries to be distinctive to each, adorned with a logo. They have in common long, thick stems and a wide mouth, as well as some kind of etching at the bottom of the bowl to produce bubbles and keep a frothy head. This provides strong aromas as you sip.

*Stemmed abbey goblet*

Use for: Abbey Dubbel.

## Tulip Glassware

Tulip glasses are designed to retain a frothy head and maintain aromas for as long as it takes to drink the multiflavored, malty beer with layers of taste profiles.

*Tulip glass*

Use for: Abbey Tripel, Saison, Biere de Garde, Lambic, Gueze, Flemish Brown and Red.

## Snifter

The large round bowl of the snifter glass is excellent for "big" beers that are more than 8 percent ABV and that you want to warm in your hand over a period of sipping. The inward taper at the top traps the aroma you want to enjoy throughout.

*Snifter*

Use for: Russian Imperial Stout, Strong Ale, Old Ale, English-style Barleywine, Imperial or Double IPA, American Barleywine, Belgian Strong Dark, Doppelbock.

## Irish Imperial Pint

The Irish imperial pint's wide mouth tapers down to a slender base and forces a frothy head, hence the aromas last longer.

*Irish imperial pint*

Use for: Stouts of all kinds.

**TASTING TIP**

Specialty glassware from a brewery to showcase a specialty brew accommodates the particular essence of that beer. Big beers with high alcohol content are served in smaller vessels. Hybrid styles have yet to define their glassware shapes.

## Various German Beer Glassware

The following is a list of German beer glassware that is named for its shape:

- *Kelch* in German means "cup," thus its shape is cuplike and looks like a stemless goblet or chalice.

- *Krug* (or *seidel*) translates to "mug" and is the only beer glass that has a handle.

- *Willibecher,* or *becher,* is German for a glass that translates into a tumbler.

And this list of German beer glassware is named for use with a particular style of beer:

- Alt glasses are particular to the North German Altbier that traditionally is drunk in smaller portions. It is a cylindrical glass that usually holds only 0.2 to 0.3 liters and is somewhat shorter and wider than a Kolsch glass.

- Berliner Kindl Weisse glassware looks like a stemmed fish bowl. Servers usually add fruit syrups to cut the acidity and bitterness and to turn Kindl into a refreshing summer drink. Syrups like woodruff (waldmeister) turns the beer green, while raspberry (himbeere) turns the beer red. And most interestingly, with a nod to ancient history, Berliners tend to drink this concoction through a straw.

- Kolsch glassware, in the North German style, holds a lesser quantity of beer. It is more delicate than an alt glass because it's made of thinner glass and is taller. Kolsch is particular to Cologne.

# The Importance of a Clean Glass

Pouring an Artisan beer into any sparkling clean glass is better than drinking directly out of a bottle or can. A major part of the enjoyment of Artisan beer is experiencing the sight and aromas of a style. And let's face it, that foamy head and "Belgian lace" are delights stored in bottles and cans that give you pleasure as you pour, drink, and ultimately converse.

> **BREW WATCH**
>
> Think of bottles and cans purely as vessels of delivery and objects to turn into artful reuse or to recycle. I've brightened many friends' and colleagues' days by bringing them a Craft beer bottle arranged with flowers from my garden. And some of my more arts-oriented friends have gone further, restructuring beer bottles into countless other uses, from candle holders, to lamps, to even glassware.

All glassware fares best when washed separately from the regular pile of dishes. With beer glassware, this is a must. Even though it's not readily visible, dishwashers leave a layer on glasses that can affect a beer's aroma and flavor. It is best to wash beer glassware by hand, in a squeaky-clean dishpan and with a sponge or dishcloth reserved only for beer glassware. Use a mild dishwashing soap (avoid high bubbles).

It is best to use the four-step system:

1. Rinse the glass with hot water.

2. Wash in a mild soap-and-water solution.

3. Rinse again with hot water.

4. Air dry upside down on a rack.

Do not towel-dry beer glassware. Lint from even the softest towel will leave dust particles, which affects head retention. Observe how bartenders handle beer glassware. While some places have specialized glass-washing equipment, most of the time it's a pretty fast rinse, soak, rinse, dry system that keeps the bar top clear of piled-up glasses.

For sparkling-clean glassware, avoid a washing container or detergents with any trace of animal or vegetable fats. It's best to place glassware in a solution of baking soda and hot water, swish, rinse with hot water, and air dry. Clean glassware is as essential for drinking Craft beer as is clean equipment for brewing, bottling, canning, and kegging.

## The Least You Need to Know

- Beer glassware is a part of the overall experience of enjoying Artisan beer.

- The qualities of each Artisan beer style are best articulated when served in glassware designed for that style.

- Artisan beer is better drunk from a glass, not from a bottle or can.

- Beer glassware needs to be washed separately, to keep it away from greasy or soapy residues, and needs to be air dried to ward off lint.

# Pairing Beer with Food

## In This Chapter

- Bringing out the best elements of a food
- Understanding beer ingredients' balance
- Pairing foods at home and when out

Throughout history, beer has been an important participant in providing nutrition, as well as being a potable beverage. While beer remains a safe beverage of choice in some parts of the world, most of us have other safe beverage options. We personally choose Craft beer as an enhancement with food because we have learned what best pleases us.

As with brewing, pairing food and beer is an art, craft, and it demands a passion for quality on all levels. This chapter gives you a jumping off point for discovering what foods are likely to go best with your favorite Craft beer.

## Making Informed Pairing Choices

Many brewpubs and restaurants make it easy by offering pairings for us. However, when an eatery doesn't have a suggested menu, you might want to know why certain choices are best. This can also help us when we're on our own for home meals.

The following is a basic rule of thumb to start with:

> A malty Lager, with its sweeter malt accents, works well with sweetish-tasting veal, pork, turkey, and chicken. Yet if it's barbecue chicken, an American Ale is a good choice.
>
> Richer, fruity Ales stand well with heartier red meats, including beef, lamb, and game. Again, for barbecue beef, the choice might best shift to American Stouts and Porters.
>
> Lagers as a category are expected to work with spicy foods. However, because each food culture has a distinctive "spiciness" to its cuisine, each needs to be treated separately. For example, Mexican spices are robust, so a medium-bodied, slightly malt-sweet Vienna-style Lager is nice, especially with its toasty aroma and flavor coming from the crystallized malt (which also lends the beer its copper or reddish-brown color).

The same kind of care applies to the cuisines of Asia, India, Australia, Islanders, and Africa, each with its specific spices and herbs and combinations of fruits, vegetables, and meats. For example, Thai cuisine calls for an American IPA, Double or Imperial Pilsner, or Saison. The diversity of Chinese cuisine demands carefully pairing to each specific region.

**BREW WATCH**

Beer's flavor profile is a balance between sweetness and dryness, imparted by malt, and further balanced by hops' bitterness. It's the hops that will trip you up in cooking if you don't pay attention. Hoppy beers impart bitterness in cooking. If you seek richness, stick with traditional malt-centric, low-hop beers, such as Belgian and Scottish Ales, English Brown Ales, and Doppelbocks.

So it's essential to pay attention to the details and nuances of specific foods and flavors, to avoid lumping any cuisine under a general category.

## Pairing with the 5-Cs

The following 5-Cs are what Craft beer does to bring out the best elements of a food when the two are drunk and eaten togethe:.

- **Complement:** With similar taste profiles. For example, you might pair a Cream Stout or a Chocolate Stout with chocolate mousse.

- **Contrast:** With opposite taste profiles. Pair smoky barbe-cued meats with a Pale Ale.

- **Cut:** As in, to cut a rich dish. Soften the impact of a very rich food, three-meat lasagna with a light, hoppy Pilsner.

- **Cleanse:** Refers to cleansing the palate. For example, you would cleanse the French fries or pommes frites salt from your palate without washing away the salty flavors, with a Belgian Blonde Ale or Lager. The same goes for Bavarian pretzels, with a Helles, the wondrous light-colored Bavarian beer.

- **Calm:** Sweet calms sweet, and acidic calms fat and salt. A Sweet Stout mellows out a layer cake, a Sour Ale mitigates a greasy burger.

Essentially, good pairings are supposed to heighten and enhance the best qualities of both the food and the beer. You want to engage all your senses in a harmonious experience.

**BREW WATCH**

The salty German pretzel we enjoy today came about by accident. On February 11, 1839, Anton Nepomuk, a baker working at the Royal Coffee House in Munich, mistook a soda–lye solution for the sugar syrup always used to glaze pretzels. Amazingly, the customers liked the unex-pected taste, and so was born the distinctive Bavarian pretzel.

When you pair, ask yourself these questions:

- What food flavors do I want the beer to compliment or contrast?

- What beer flavors do I want the food to compliment or contrast?

- Do I want a calming affect or the opposite?

## Working with Food Elements

Basic food elements inherent in beer and food recipes work with each other to bring out the best tastes and digestive factors in the same way that dressings work with salads. For example:

**Salt:** Salt flavors in food counter acidic flavors in beer. Acidic beers include Berliner Weiss, Gueze, Lambic, and Flanders Red and Brown.

**Acidity:** You'll find these flavors especially in tomato dishes and salad dressings. Acidic foods with acidic beers mute each other so that the other food elements actually stand out.

**Sweetness:** Pairing sweetness with acidity increases the acidity, so avoid sweet and acidity (unless you want greater acidity); conversely, sweet plus sweet increases sweet, so you get more from both a malt-forward beer and a rich dessert.

**BREW WATCH**

For a beer dinner, begin pairing lower-alcohol beers with the appetizer and soup, then move up a notch with the main course, and close with a bigger beer for dessert. Serve smaller portions of food and beer—4 ounce glassware is best.

**Fat:** Acidic beer cuts fat and helps your taste buds sense more of the food flavors.

**Spice and Herbs:** Yeast-forward beers bring out more of the spices and herbs in foods.

**Heat:** Malt-forward beers soothe the palate from the heat of chili peppers and hot pepper flakes.

# Beer Ingredients Affecting the Relationship with Food

Each beer ingredient has a character of its own. If the balance is toward malt, that beer will be sweeter than a beer with a higher bittering hop content. The temperature of roasting will affect the color of the grain. As a rule of thumb, darker color beers have fuller body, but are not necessarily higher in alcohol content than lighter beers. It's the balance between ingredients that determines how a beer and a food pair:

**Malt:** Grains singly or in combinations give sweetness and fullness, color/hue, and aroma. That's why malt-centric beers taste good with desserts.

**Hops:** Singly or in combinations give bitterness or aroma; can be wet-hopped or dry-hopped. Bittering hops are added to the recipe to give the beer a bitter quality. Aromatic hops are in the recipe to give the beer its aroma. Some beers are single-hopped, most have a combination of bittering and aromatic hops. Hop-centric beers stand up to spiced and fatty foods.

**Yeast:** The yeast used determines whether the beer is an Ale, a Lager, or a hybrid; imbues flavors. Ales have more layers of flavor than do Lagers, so an Ale can be a fine companion for multi-layered foods such as stews while a more straightforward Lager is lovely with a simple grilled cheese sandwich.

**Water:** In its natural state, water determines style. It can be treated to achieve the level of hardness or softness desired, and trace elements of minerals can be added to affect taste.

**Additives:** These include fruits, herbs, spices, and other grains, such as corn flakes.

**Carbonation:** A sip of beer with carbonation gently scrubs the tongue and readies your mouth for the next bite.

# A General Guide for Pairing

Here is a starting point for you to work from for your home cooking as well as for eating out:

**Amber Ale:** Its malt-forward character complements pizza, sandwiches, and hearty soups (beans, peas, chilis), and cuts through barbecue and Mexican foods.

**American Wheat Ale, Blonde Ale, Golden Ale, Lagers (lightly hopped):** Balanced between malts and hops, these are thirst quenchers (often referred to as "lawn mower brews" because they're perfect after yard work). They also contrast or cut "hot" foods.

**Barley Wines, Old Ales:** Strong beers with a hefty malt backbone to support the hops, these winter brews beg for strong, hard cheeses or a chunk of really dark chocolate, or can simply be enjoyed alone as dessert.

**Belgians:** A light Wheat beer's aromatic spices and touch of citrus are perfect with a nutty Gruyere. Blonde or Golden Ale is a variation on Pale Ale; it's sometimes made with a Pilsner malt and sometimes spiced with coriander. It is especially good with delicate recipes and fish. Lambics, made with nonmalted wheat and fermented with wild, airborne yeast, have a tart, crisp, dry flavor that complements light, white meat dishes and contrasts well with sweet desserts.

**Bitter Ale, Pale Ale, India Pale Ale, German/Bohemian Pilsners:** Hop-forward beers, these cut through fried-food greasiness, stand up to pickled foods (pickled eggs are in jars atop bars in Germany), and complement highly seasoned foods, seafood of all kinds, and red meats.

**Bock, Dark Lager, Vienna Lager, Oktoberfest/Maarzen:** Lighter than Ales, these beers make a nice change from the Ambers that are all-around food beers. They are, of course, the perfect pairing with hot, soft German pretzels and mustards, and hearty German meat dishes. Doppelbocks, which tilt toward maltiness, complement spice-centric desserts such as bread puddings, gingerbread, pumpkin pie, and carrot and spice cakes.

**Cream or Sweet Stout, Imperial Stout:** Malt forward, these are perfect with chocolate and desserts of any kind.

**Dunkelweiss, Weissbier:** Yeast forward, their flavors are best enjoyed with delicate cream soups, light cheese (goat), primavera pastas, grilled and steamed vegetables, and rice dishes.

**English or American Brown Ales:** Balanced toward hops, these pair well with smoked fish and smoked meats such as sausages, and with hamburgers.

**Fruit Beers, Lambics:** Their range of tartness to sourness requires careful pairing to cover the range of complement, contrast, or cut. Some fruit beers seem to be fated for fruit desserts; Lambics and dark chocolate are totally elegant. Some fruit-glazed Chinese dishes are perfect with fruit beers. Both styles satisfy alone as a beer dessert or with a cheese/fruit/cracker platter for an informal get-together.

**Porter, Dry, or Oatmeal Stout:** Malt forward, these are favorites with shepherd's pies, stews, roast meats of any kind, and steamed oysters. As with Brown Ales, think strong cheeses.

## The Least You Need to Know

- Beer is a food that adds nutrition and calories to a meal or a snack. Factor that into whatever you are cooking and eating.

- Ask basic questions when cooking and pairing: 1) What food flavors do I want the beer to complement or contrast? 2) What beer flavors do I want the food to complement or contrast? Be aware of intensities—very mild, mild, big, very big—and pair accordingly.

- Artisan beer and Artisan cheese are naturals, so get creative with pairings for something extraordinary. Allow the beer to show off every bite of cheese. Be aware of the right temperature for serving each beer and each cheese. Ask questions when you shop.

# Hosting a Craft Beer Event

# 12

## In This Chapter

- Determining who you will invite
- Getting to know your attendees
- Preparing for the big event
- Picking your beer theme

When you plan a beer tasting event, decide what you want to accomplish. Do you want to tie into a civic event, enjoy the growing variety of beer and food possibilities, acquire abilities to enjoy beer on many levels, or simply kick back and have fun? This chapter brings together all you've learned so far and opens ideas for enjoying Craft beer in companionship with colleagues, friends, and family.

## Who's Coming to the Tasting?

When putting together a beer tasting in your home, the primary question you want to ask is, who you are inviting? You need to have a good understanding of the people you want to invite and think about whether they will enjoy themselves with the beer you've chosen.

> **DEFINITIONS**
>
> A **Certified Cicerone** is an individual who has passed a series of rigor-
> ous examinations regarding Artisan beer to qualify as a knowledgeable
> server, wait staff, bartender, or beer company representative (rep).
> Many brewpubs, taverns, restaurants, and beer-distributing companies
> now require Cicerone training. Further study qualifies an individual as a
> Master Cicerone.

If you don't know your guests' level of beer knowledge, the best way
to determine what they might like is to give them a short questionnaire. *Certified Ciscerone*, Cari Crowe, suggests a beer quiz to help
you assess your guests' level of beer knowledge so you can determine
the kind of information you need to provide at the tasting event
you are planning. Have each person you invite to your beer tasting
party complete this Basic Beer Knowledge Quiz (answers are in
parenthesis—don't provide them those, of course):

1. On a scale of 1 to 10—1 being Least and 10 being Most—
   what do you feel is your level of beer knowledge?

2. What are your favorite style(s) of beer?

3. What are the four main ingredients of beer? (malted barley,
   water, yeast, hops)

4. What are the two main groupings of beer? (Lagers and Ales)

5. If a beer is described as "hoppy," what does that tell you
   about that beer? (It is a bitter beer and can have flavors like
   grapefruit or lemons, tropical fruit, or grass.)

6. If a beer is described as "malty," what does that tell you
   about that beer? (It may have flavors like caramel, chocolate,
   or coffee.)

7. What has happened to a beer if it is "skunky"? (It has been
   exposed to too much light—fluorescent or ultraviolet.)

8. Can you age beer? (Yes!)

9. What does ABV mean? (Alcohol by volume)

10. What does IBU mean? (International bitterness unit)

These are pretty telling questions. Some are more direct, as with questions #1 and #2, but the rest test basic beer knowledge.

You can send this questionnaire to your guests in an email along with the invitation. Make sure they understand that this will be fun—no final test involved—but they will likely learn something along the way.

**BREW WATCH**

Beer parties go back to the beginning of civilization. According to an inscription on a stele found during an archeological search, in 879 B.C.E., the Assyrian king Assurnasirapli II gave a stupendous banquet as part of the inauguration of his new palace. According to author A. Kirk Grayson in his book *Assyrian Rulers of the Early First Millennium B.C. 1119–859* (University of Toronto Press, 1991), there were 10,000 containers of beer for no fewer than 69,574 guests.

# Perceived Beer Knowledge and Preferences

The average person knows a little bit about beer. Everyone generally has personal favorite styles. Still, people have a lot of preconceived notions about beer and accept some old wives' tales about beer as common knowledge.

Ever heard that Bock beers are made from the dregs from the bottom of the tanks? How about that if you buy cold beer at a store and transport it in your car, it will skunk, or not taste as good? Both of those are commonly heard beer "facts" that are completely and utterly false.

On the other hand, some people know a great deal about beer. Questions 3–10 determine this. This 10-point "test" is a good way to learn the comfort level of your friends without coming off as judgmental.

**TASTING TIP**

In case someone attends your beer event as a friend of a friend or a spouse or partner and announces, "I don't like beer," you nevertheless can learn orally what it is this person does like to drink and guide this person to try a beer with a matching profile. For example, coffee drinkers find a Coffee Stout appealing. Wine drinkers usually enjoy a beer made with fruit or a Wheat beer. If someone says, "I don't like the bitter taste of beer" steer them away from hoppy beers such as IPAs and offer them a mild English Brown Ale. People who prefer sweet soft drinks most likely will find a malt-centric beer pleasing. If someone has always drunk a macro-produced lite/light beer, offer a gateway beer into the world of Craft such as Amber Ale or an Amber Lager. If adamant non-Craft beer drinking guests arrive offer them any other beverage on hand and invite them into the conversation nonetheless.

# Preparing Your Guests to Taste

As everyone is arriving, remind all guests to refrain from the following activities for at least 15 to 30 minutes before the tasting begins:

- Smoking

- Eating strongly flavored food

- Eating or drinking hot foods

- Eating breath mints or chewing gum

- Applying strong-smelling hand or body lotion, perfume, or cologne

- Washing hands with strong-smelling soap

Some of these "activities" are determined by what you, as the host, serve to your guests. If you offer garlic dip and cracked black pepper crackers, you are not helping to set the stage. Perhaps a mild cheese and plain water crackers might be a better offering. In addition, your powder room should not be full of incense and fragrant hand soaps. Certified beer judges are careful to keep out any environmental aromas or foods that will take away from their ability to fully appreciate the qualities of the glass of beer in their hand.

## What to Provide Your Guests

Here are some other items you will want to provide your guests:

- Clipboards or individual notepads

- Pencils with erasers

- Napkins and small serving plates (forks, knives, spoons)

- Snacks (unsalted crackers are best; avoid greasy, overly salty snacks)

- Water and glasses for cleansing the palate

- Bottle openers

- Tasting glasses (4-oz. size is a good choice)

- Tasting sheets (see Appendix C for sample sheets that match the party suggestions later in this chapter)

- Profile description of each beer sample (make copies for your guests to take home)

In case you're wondering how much beer you need to purchase, the following is a good rule of thumb for sampling: 3 people can share a bottle or can of beer; 12 people can share a growler. Make sure you plan accordingly because you don't want to run out of beer at your own party.

> **TASTING TIP**
>
> Here are some brewing-related decoration ideas. Place some hops in a clear glass bowl, provide samples of different grains and malts, and display unique Craft beer posters. Consider displaying some beer memorabilia, maps showing the centers of great beer traditions, and you will want to provide flags of the countries represented.

## Review the Tasting Techniques

Make sure everyone has clear glasses so they can confidently evaluate their beer. If you don't have good tasting glasses, I recommend using a clear wine glass, especially with a shorter stem, or a clear water goblet. This will give you a wide opening from which to see, swirl, and smell the beer. Review the beer-tasting techniques you learned in Chapter 8 with your guests (refer to the section "The Six Steps to a Proper Tasting"):

- SEE

  Ask the following questions:

  Is the beer clean looking or cloudy?

  Does it have a nice soft haze, or are there particles clumped together?

  Is the color lighter, darker, or in between?

  Is the head creamy, frothy, or not very existent?

- SWIRL

  Gently swirl your beer in the glass, making sure you don't let it slosh out the sides. This both agitates the beer and warms it, releasing scents and possibly hidden flavors.

- SMELL

  Place your nose inside the glass, above the beer, making sure not to stick your nose into the beer or froth. Take a deep breath and observe what you smell.

> **TASTING TIP**
>
> Before you begin pouring, be sure to bring each beer to the correct serving temperature for the desired amount of time.

- SIP

  When you first try a beer, don't gulp it. Take a sip, and run it across your tongue and throughout your mouth before swallowing. This allows the beer to coat your tongue and cover all the flavor-sensing regions of your tongue.

- SWALLOW

  We swallow beer because, to detect bitter, the beer has to reach the back of our tongue. Since bitter is a good trait in beer, we have to swallow it to reach that area of the tongue. With wine, since bitter is not a positive trait, spitting out the wine is acceptable.

Take time to go through each step, allowing for conversation about what each guest is detecting, experiencing, feeling, but remember that a beer's aroma is volatile so you want to sniff very early in the process. You don't have to hurry any of the other steps. And remind guests to sip water between each beer to cleanse the palate from one beer to the next. Eating a water cracker is equally good.

# Choosing a Tasting Party Theme

Themes for a beer-tasting party can vary greatly, so choosing one is both easy and hard. I suggest choosing a theme tailored to the people you are inviting.

If your friends are novice Craft beer drinkers, here are a few suggestions for getting Artisan beer into their hands:

- During a sporting event. Try exploring beers from the cities where the teams are located.

- Surrounding the release of a new or favorite TV show. Provide an assortment of beers from where the show takes place.

- When entertaining at a holiday party. Offer up seasonal beers that are released only during that time of year.

If you are inviting more experienced imbibers, try the following suggestions:

- Theme the tasting around beers you rarely find in your area—perhaps beers you brought back from a recent trip.

- Theme the tasting around similar beer styles. Perhaps compare styles from different countries, regions, or even continents.

- Theme the tasting around food. Perhaps pair the beers with some "unexpected" foods that go against the usual "style" (not necessarily the usual combinations). Talk about how the beer and food interact to bring out qualities not usually perceived.

Another fun theme is a "blind taste test" style party. You can give all your guests typed statements that describe all different kinds of beer. Set up a tasting station where multiple beers are poured into glasses. Have your guests study and taste each beer, and then have them put their name on their "statements" and drop them in the bowl of the beer they think it matches. This can be lots of fun. Make sure you have a prize for whoever correctly identifies the most beers. Present the winner with a unique bottle opener, a fun beer coozie, or perhaps another copy of this *Complete Idiot's Guide*!

# Tasting Party Theme 1: "In Good Taste"

Arrange a tasting event featuring a homebrew supply store owner, homebrewer, bottle store owner, professional brewer, certified beer judge, or Certified Ciscerone whom you have met in your personal quest. Ask your featured guest to bring a beer that is typical of a particular style. The plan is to walk everyone through the unique profile of one specific style to show how the aroma, appearance, flavor, body, and finish/aftertaste are readily identifiable with this style. You want to share what in this beer's recipe makes it a sterling example of what a beer judge is looking for in, say, an American Pale Ale or an Irish Red or a Belgian Wit. Be sure to allow time before sampling to get acquainted with the ingredients; this will help the expert guide you through the profile of the beer.

Craft beer professionals are dedicated to "growing the category." I have not yet met anyone in Craft brewing who is unwilling to be part of an event to help educate consumers. They might ask you to come to their location rather than come to your home, but by limiting the request to one style for a small group, you are within bounds for an event at a minimal cost ranging between $5 to $15 per guest, depending on the number of samples and food you also are providing. Learn from the experts what foods they recommend to best serve with each beer style.

Best is to have your expert provide samples of the malts and hops used in the recipe of the "showcase" beer, and to describe the special properties each ingredient imparts to make this beer a recognized standard. Smell and taste the raw ingredients. Keep these smells and tastes in mind for when you are sampling the beer. The yeast used is equally important, but yeast is hard to carry around, so believe what you are being told without seeing, smelling, and tasting yeast. The same is true for water. You will want to be aware of what qualities in the water used by the brewer are particularly suited to this style of beer.

Review the BJCP standards for this style. Note how close this "standard" beer is to the style guidelines. You can access these guidelines at www.bjcp.ot/stylecenter.php.

After sampling the "example to style" beer, taking notes, and having a conversation about what you are all experiencing, you will want to serve three or four samples (one at a time) of other beers in this particular style.

The prepared "In Good Taste" Tasting Sheets in Appendix C have space for five beers. Your goal is to determine which is closest to the showcase style, to choose which you each personally like best, and to articulate why. Allow time for conversation and questions as you sample each beer.

Consider planning a series of single style events so you can become proficient in the nuances of beer styles. This is the kind of event that opens possibilities for future visits to local establishments that have several brands of a style. In this way, you can broaden and deepen your expertise as you and your friends come to know beers by style.

# Tasting Party Theme 2: "Mix 'n' Match"

Plan an event where you serve one or two appetizers with a choice of four beers. Confer with the sales clerk at the store where you are making your bottle and can purchases, and with the server/brewer at the brewery where you are making your growler (or bottle/can) purchases. They all are happy to share their knowledge about beer and food pairing. Use the knowledge you acquired from the event previously described to plan the specific taste profile of the featured foods with a style of beer. Allow time to talk about which combinations you and your guests like best. What makes a combination outstanding or not a favorite?

The prepared "Mix 'n' Match" Tasting Sheets in Appendix C have space for four beers. Remember to choose a food-and-beer combination to give you opportunities to learn about pairings for similar tastes and opposite tastes.

You can plan similar events for one or two salads with a choice of four beers, one or two desserts with a choice of four beers, or an entree with a choice of four beers. The value of serving a single food item with a choice of beers is that you and your friends can concentrate on learning pairings without a lot of distractions. These private events open you and your friends to get the most out of restaurant-prepared "beer dinners."

# Tasting Party Theme 3: "Great Traditions"

Create a tasting event around one Great Beer Tradition, or plan a series to include the following:

- The British Ale tradition
- The Belgian Ale tradition
- The Czech–German–Vienna Lager tradition

Or look at new traditions, including these:

- Canadian beers by region
- U.S. beers by region
- Australia and New Zealand beers

Try featuring an authentic style in a great beer tradition, along with two or three beers made in the United States that are based on that style. For example, try an authentic imported Vienna Lager with two or three U.S. Craft-brewed Vienna-style Lagers. Look for the differences between an imported beer in a traditional style and an

American Craft version of that style. Allow time for conversation. The prepared "Great Traditions" Tasting Sheets in Appendix C have space for four beers.

# Tasting Party Theme 4: "Beers by Season"

Each seasonal beer is brewed during the previous season, to be properly fermented and fresh:

- Winter seasonals are brewed in the fall.

- Spring seasonals are brewed in the winter.

- Summer seasonals are brewed in the spring.

- Fall seasonals are brewed in the summer.

Winter seasonals, usually dark and hearty, also include big beers such as Barleywines that require at least a year of aging, so they are brewed a year in advance. And everyone seems to have a favorite holiday or Christmas recipe that defies categorizing. Stouts, Porters, Winter Wheats, Scotch Ale, Old Ale, Rauchbier. Spring styles move toward the lighter spectrum and include the traditions of St. Patrick's Day and Easter, and the harvesting of first fruits.

Every season, you can have a party where each person attending brings an appropriate beer and food to share, and prepares a little presentation about that beer and food. The prepared "Beers by Season" Tasting Sheets in Appendix C have space for four beers.

# Additional Tasting Party Ideas

When you and your friends have gotten pretty good at "knowing" about Artisan beers and foods as pairings, kick back and just have fun. Here are some themes to build a beer and food party where everyone pitches in:

- Plan a tasting event around beers made with a single hop or single malt. The point here is to get to know the qualities of a specific hop or malt.

- Before or after a sporting event, each guest brings a food dish and beer choice that best exemplifies the teams that played. The guests describe why they made this choice, and all the other guests "score" the choices. The winner gets a prize for the best game/player, food/beer pairing.

- Before or after a concert, each guest brings a food dish and beer choice that best exemplifies the music and musicians heard. The guests describe why they made this choice, and the other guests "score" the choices. The winner gets a prize for the best music/musician, food/beer pairing.

- When focusing on a civic issue, each guest brings a dish and a beer choice to best bring the issue (and its pros and cons) to a worthy closure.

- Plan a tasting party for beers to match literary genres. This can be for a reading club or just for fun. Have guests decide what beers go best with adventure stories, detective novels, travel books, British novels, and so on. Each person brings a beer and food item to share and tells why they are appropriate for the genre of literature.

- Plan an evening to explore philosophical questions. Everyone brings beer and food to share based on a chosen topic. What brews and foods inspire specific topics?

- Plan a PBS "Masterpiece-Watching Party," with beers and foods matched to the program on TV.

- Plan a locally sourced Artisan food and beer party based on specific combinations, such as these:

  - Beers and appetizers

  - Beers and cheese

  - Beers and fruits

- Beers and specific meats

- Beers and food made with each of the beers

Review what you have learned in all the preceding chapters of this book. You should feel confident that you are ready to share your personal enthusiasm for Artisan beer and food. Keep in mind that you don't always have to plan your own parties. You can find fun events with beer and food all around your community. And remember, we savor Craft beer for its qualities as a beverage to satisfy all our senses. Thus, we drink responsibly for enjoyment.

## The Least You Need to Know

- Determine whether the people you invite to your party will enjoy themselves with the beer you've chosen. Try a questionnaire or quiz to learn more.

- A tasting party with a single style helps you and your friends learn that style in depth. Learn one style at a time and move on. It's a life-long quest, not a cram course.

- Be careful to keep out any environmental aromas or foods that will take away from your guests' ability to fully appreciate the qualities of the glass of beer in their hands.

- People in the Craft beer industry are eager to help educate consumers. Befriend them and learn from them.

# Glossary

**Abbey beers**   Traditional styles distinctive to Belgian monastic breweries that are protected by law. These styles brewed by anyone else must be labeled "Abbey-style."

**ABV (alcohol by volume)**   The standard in the United States indicating the alcohol level in beer, measured by percent. The higher the percent number, the higher the alcohol.

**ABW (alcohol by weight)**   An alternate measure indicating the alcohol level in beer. Convert ABW to ABV by multiplying the ABW percent by 1.25.

**adjunct**   Anything added to the brewing process besides malted barley or wheat, hops, yeast, and water to change the aroma, flavor, or body of the beer.

**Ale**   One of the two major types of beer; the other is Lager. Ale preceded the brewing of Lager. It is fermented at high temperatures, and the yeast rises to the top. Aging takes a minimum of two weeks to a month. Ales generally are full-bodied, with fruity characteristics, and include a wide range of styles and substyles. The Artisan Ales you are most likely to find served include Barleywine, Pale Ale, Porter, Stout, and Wheat beer.

**Amber Lager**   Considered an all-around refreshing beer. American Amber Lagers generally have a higher hop content than European Amber Lagers, thus higher bitterness to cut through the condiments of the quintessential American hamburger, while also a good contrast with sweet foods.

**American Pale Lager** A Lager that is light in color and body, and thin in flavor.

**appearance** The way a beer looks in a glass. A beer is described by its color or hue, the color and size of its head, and whether it is filtered or nonfiltered (thus, clear or hazy).

**aroma** The ingredients and the process of brewing contribute to the aroma of beer. It is what we first encounter immediately upon pouring, and it gives us an immediate impression about the beer. Each style has a distinctive aroma.

**aroma hops** Different from hops to impart bitterness, aroma hops add a bouquet quality to beer.

**aromatic hops (or Noble hops)** These are distinctive varieties with unique qualities for both aroma and flavoring when used in the brewing process.

**barley** One of the four primary ingredients of most Artisan beers. Malted barley suited for each style provides particular aroma, color, and flavor.

**Barleywine (or Barley Wine)** A strong Ale beer style, with 8 to 12 percent ABV, traced to ancient Greece. Bass No. 1 Ale was the first Barley Wine marketed in England (around 1870). American Barley Wine typically is hoppier and more bitter.

**barrel (or cask)** The wooden container in which some beers are aged (hence, "barrel aged"), traditionally in used whiskey or wine barrels. The beer thus inherits qualities of the whiskey or wine along with the qualities of the wood.

**Bavarian Weissbier** A Wheat beer brewed with a special yeast strain that imparts a range of flavors, starting with bananas and cloves, and growing into the aroma and taste of green apples, bubble gum, wood smoke, and vanilla. Wheat beer can be traced back to ancient Babylonia.

**beer bubbles**   Carbonation occurs when carbon dioxide bubbles are "trapped" at the end of fermentation. This natural process is called bunging.

**beer cans**   Originated in 1933 by the Krueger Brewing Company of Newark, New Jersey, and made of heavy tin or steel. Aluminum cans came into use in 1959 by Coors Brewing Company. Newer-type beer cans now have recloseable screw caps and resemble the shape of a bottle, to hold higher-alcohol beers that are usually shared between several people.

**Belgian lace (or Brussels lace)**   The foam that clings to the side of a glass as the beer's head recedes while you drink.

**Belgian Wheat beer (or Witbier)**   A pale-colored, unfiltered, light-bodied beer with refreshing acidity. Compare its orange peel and coriander notes to German Wheat beer or Weissbier, with its aromas of clove and banana.

**bittering hops**   Impart the bitter taste.

**Bock beer**   A style of Lager first brewed in the city of Einbeck, in northern Germany, often marketed with a goat on the label. *Bock* is the German word for "goat." At 6 to 8 percent ABV, these are "strong beers," with a malt backbone to balance the hops. There are substyles for greater strength/alcohol, such as Doppelbock and Triple Bock.

**body**   How the beer feels in the mouth. Some feel it is a sensation of fullness coming from an abundance of malt proteins. Some feel it is a thin feel because of a sparseness of malts.

**body and soul commodity**   This refers to malt not only supplying a Craft beer's backbone to provide pleasing balance with the hops, but equally to the beer's essential link with the culture (the place of origin) associated with that style.

**bottle-conditioned**   A second fermentation by yeast left in the bottle.

**bouquet** See *nose*.

**Brewers Association (B.A.)** The trade organization to which most brewers belong. The B.A. sets standards and runs the Great American Beer Festival where brewers are awarded for best brews and sustained quality. It also provides information about beers and brewing to brewers and the general public.

**brewing** The specific process of making wort (the liquid from the heating of malt and water), boiling wort with hops, and adding yeast to ferment the liquid into beer.

**brewpub** A brewery where an Artisan beer is served on tap and food is part of the operation; it differs from a production brewery, where beer is brewed exclusively for sale off the premises. Some brewpubs also bottle, can, and fill growlers and kegs for takeaway or for sale elsewhere. Some production breweries have a tasting room. Some "upscale" brewpubs serve Artisan food and market themselves as a gastropub or a brasserie.

**British bitter** The term for beer served in British pubs directly from the cask in which it has been conditioning, along with the yeast. It is unfiltered, has little to no carbonation, and is served at cellar temperatures (not refrigerated).

**Brussels lace** See *Belgian lace*.

**bung (or plug)** Traditionally, the wooden stopper that caps the hole in a barrel through which a brewer fills or empties the barrel.

**bunging** See *beer bubbles*.

**carbonation** The process of dissolving carbon dioxide in a liquid. With beer, carbonation provides a sensation of smoothness.

**cask** See *barrel*.

**Certified Beer Judge** An individual who has passed a series of rigorous examinations to qualify to judge beers according to style at beer competitions. The Beer Judge Certification Program was founded in 1985 and administers the BJCP exam worldwide (www. bjcp.org). Certified judges act as instructors in formal classes for people desiring to gain certification, resembling a guild system where knowledge and information is passed down. In addition, trainees work alongside certified judges to gain experience in knowing what to look for in each style and how to fill out the forms to help a brewer brew better. BJCP is managed by an elected board of directors and has directors heading up each of its operations. Higher levels of certification require greater knowledge and specific hours of experience in judging.

**Certified Cicerone**   An individual who has passed a series of rigorous examinations regarding Artisan beer to qualify as a knowledgeable server, wait staff, bartender, or beer company representative (rep). Many brewpubs, taverns, restaurants, and beer-distributing companies now require Cicerone training. Further study qualifies an individual as a Master Cicerone.

**cold filtering**   The universal process by which unwanted yeast and protein are removed from the beer before serving, bottling, or canning.

**Craft brewery**   As defined by the Brewers Association (B.A.), a U.S. brewery that is "small, independent, and traditional." To be classified as a "regional Craft brewery" by the B.A., a brewery must either possess "an all-malt flagship or [have] at least 50 percent of its volume in either all-malt beers or in beers which use adjuncts to enhance rather than lighten flavor."

**diacetyl**   A compound that imparts a butterscotch-like taste to beer. This signals that the beer has flaws. For example, if the beer feels very slippery, like eating a pat of melting butter. A small amount is tolerable in English Pale Ales.

**Dortmunder**   Originating in the German city of Dortmund, it is a style of Pilsner that is darker and sweeter.

**dry**   In a dry beer, hops bitterness overrides malt sweetness.

**dry hopping**   In the brewing process, adding hops in the fermenter or in the keg after fermentation. Dry hopping adds to the "hoppy" flavor and aroma without increasing bitterness.

**Dunkel**   This means "dark" in German. It is a style of barley beer that is reddish-brown in hue, with a particularly smooth mouthfeel; it imparts caramel, coffee, and nutty flavors.

**Dunkles Weissbier (or Dunkles Weizen)**   This is a dark version of a Wheat beer; *dunkel* is German for "dark."

**emmer**   A wild and cultivated wheat of antiquity. Now it is a relic crop found in mountainous regions and grown in Italy, where it is known as faro and protected by law. Emmer has expanded nutritional qualities, along with the ability to grow where other crops fail because of poor soil and climate.

**English Stouts**   So dark they might look black, with a rich chocolaty taste and a touch of coffee that comes from the highly roasted barley called chocolate malt. Compare with Irish Stouts, which tend to be bitter and dry.

**expiration date**   Fresh is best with beer. While some high-alcohol beers are brewed to be cellared under ideal conditions and to be drunk even ten years after bottling, most beers should be drunk within four to six months of the date on the bottle. Beer quality deteriorates with exposure to heat and light.

**fermentation**   When making beer, this is the process of yeast metabolizing sugar into carbon dioxide and alcohol.

**fermenter**   At the end of the brewing process, the wort is transferred to the fermenter tank to complete its cycle into becoming beer.

**finishing hops**   Added to the wort at the end of the boil to give the beer a hoppy aroma without bitterness.

**flavor**   The taste characteristics of a beer that come from the type and amount of malt, yeast, hops, and, in some cases, the quality of the water.

**German Wheat beer (or Weissbier)**   A light-colored beer with a specialized yeast that imparts aromas of clove and banana. Compare with the orange peel and coriander notes of Belgian Wheat beer, or Witbier.

**grist**   A brewer's term for the grains that are stirred into hot water in the mash tun to make the mash.

**growler**   A late-nineteenth-century/early-twentieth-century container (usually a tin bucket or pail) used to carry beer from a tavern to the home. In the United States, it came back into use after the repeal of Prohibition. While there are many fanciful explanations for the name *growler*, it is generally accepted that the name comes from the growling sound of carbon dioxide bubbles escaping from the vents on the cover as the pail was jostled during carrying. Most Artisan breweries and brewpubs offer carryout in glass bottles still called growlers, and some offer a smaller size in plastic, dubbed howlers.

**gruit (or grut)**   An herb mixture (usually in a bundle) used for bittering and flavoring beer. It was used before hops became the preferred ingredient. Gruit originally was a combination of herbs including sweet gale, mugwort, yarrow, ground ivy, horehound, and heather. Different herbs were used to gain distinctive flavors.

**hefe**   The German word for yeast.

**Hefeweizen (or Hefeweissbier)**   This is a German-style unfiltered, cloudy, frothy beer that is bottled or kegged with the yeast in suspension. In German, *hefe* means "yeast" and *weizen* means "wheat."

**homebrewing**   From its beginnings, beer has been brewed in homes; from there, it became commercialized. During U.S. Prohibition in 1919, homebrewing and commercial brewing became illegal (except for making a "malt brew" of under 0.5 percent ABV). A clerical error left homebrewing out of the bill legalizing home winemaking with the repeal of Prohibition in 1933. Not until 1978, with President Jimmy Carter signing the law, was homebrewing for personal use made legal. However, states retain a right to ban homebrewing, and some still do. Homebrewers and professional brewers follow the same steps as professional brewers to ensure highest sanitary conditions, quality of ingredients, and attention to detail for brewing steps and storage. Quality and consistency combine with innovation. Homebrewers are credited with bringing back many styles lost to the rush to embrace mass-produced beers with only one flavor profile.

**honey wine**   See *mead.*

**hops**   Flowers of a climbing vine that brewers have used since about 600 C.E. as a preservative and to give beer a bitter, clean taste to balance out the malt sweetness. American varieties are considered more citric and piney than are European hops. Aroma hops are bred to impart aroma; high-alpha hops are bred to impart maximum bittering qualities. Noble hops impart both bittering and aromatic character to a brew. Hops can be used fresh right after their fall harvest, as dried whole hops, or made into pellets and dried. Hops varieties are developed in laboratories and on hops farms dedicated to the Craft/Artisan beer industry.

**IBU (international bitterness unit)**   IBU measures the bitterness of a beer, which, of course, comes from the addition of hops. The higher the IBU percent, the "hoppier," or more bitter, the beer tastes. For example, India Pale Ales (IPA) have a high IBU concentration.

**ice beer (or Eisbock)**   Made by freezing the beer, the process is thought to have been "discovered" by a tavern keeper in Bavaria, Germany, when he left a keg of beer in the snow. Eisbock in Germany is a dark, very concentrated, full-flavor beer with high alcohol content. American Ice Beers are less alcoholic and less flavorful because the ice shavings are not removed, thus they are thinner.

**India Pale Ale**   Originally brewed in eighteenth-century Great Britain to send by ship to India, whose temperature and water conditions were not at that time suitable for brewing. To survive the months-long ocean voyage, the Pale Ale brew was highly hopped. The practice continues even though high-alcohol IPAs are brewed and drunk locally worldwide, including in India.

**Irish Stout**   Also known as Dry Stout (Leann Dubh means "black beer" in Irish), has a very rich, dark color, with a bitter, coffeelike taste. Compared with English or American Stout, Irish Stout is deemed "light in flavor."

**keg**   Traditionally made of wood by a cooper and used to carry gunpowder, nails, and liquids, including beer. Beer (or other carbonated beverage) kegs are now made of stainless steel and sometimes of aluminum. Keg sizes are not standardized. Generally, a keg is smaller than a barrel. A smaller keg is called a pony keg.

**kegerator**   A refrigerated keg that keeps unpasteurized beer safe and tasting good for about six months.

**King Gambrinus**   Revered in Europe as the Patron Saint of Beer. Several legends surround the persona and the sainthood. Google the name, and enjoy the multiple stories.

**Kristallweissbier (or Kristallweizen)**   This Wheat beer is filtered Weissbier, so it looks clear; *kristall* means "clear" in German.

**La Bière Blanche (or White Beer)**   This is the French name for Wheat beer.

**labeorphilist (or labologist)**   A person who collects beer bottle labels. Paper labels on beer bottles came into use around 1840.

**lactic acid**   A tart acid that infects beer; its presence indicates that a beer is spoiled.

**Lager**   The second major style of beer (Ale is the first). Lagers were developed in Germany during the eighteenth century. Beers were fermented using cool temperatures and a special Lager yeast; they were then stored cold from a number of weeks up to months, and sometimes a year, before being served. *Lager* in German means "to store." The Lagers you are most likely to find include American Pale Lager, Bock, Munchener Helles, Oktoberfest, and Pilsner.

**Lambic**   Considered the oldest style of beer. Lambic is traced to the Belgian town of Lembeek. These are Wheat Ales brewed naturally in open containers to allow fermentation with wild yeast. They have a complex favor, with fruity and sour elements. When wheat was co-opted expressly for baking bread, barley became the choice grain for brewing.

**lauter tun**   The vessel used to strain the liquid wort off the spent grains after the mashing process.

**"low-point" beer (or "three-two beer" or "3 point 2 brew")**
Beer with 3.2 percent alcohol by weight (ABW), equivalent to 4 percent alcohol by volume (ABV). Licensing sales of low-point beer fall under categories different from licensing sales for higher-alcohol beers.

**malster**   The person who transforms barley seeds into malt for brewing.

**malting**   The process that turns raw barley into malt for brewing. The three-step process involves (1) steeping the hard barley seeds in water and then aerating, (2) allowing the barley to germinate very briefly, and (3) drying and curing/heating in a kiln. The temperature and length of roasting time determines the color and the caramelized and roasted flavors of the malt (thus, the color and flavor of the beer).

**mash tun**   Pronounced as "ton," this is a large specialized/insulated container the brewer uses to mix mash with water and to keep the mixture, called the mash, at a steady (or increasing) temperature for at least an hour while the grain's enzymes turn into sugars.

Commercial brewers favor a copper kettle. Homebrewers use stew pots, plastic buckets, or any other such containers to make the mash.

**mead**   Also called Honey Wine. Mead is an ancient beverage with no exact known beginning. It is made by fermenting honey with water and generally is the color of the honey. Some mead makers add fruit, herbs, and hops, and some add light malt that is strained out.

**microbrewery**   A brewery that produces a limited amount of beer. In the United Kingdom, the term refers to "operating under the U.K. Progressive Beer Duty threshold." Cask-conditioned bitter is the most common brew made under this threshold. According to state and federal laws in the United States, the upper limit in the United States is 6 million beer barrels (bbl). The Brewers Association (BA) defines a microbrewery as producing between 15,000 and 20,000 bbl per year and meeting rigid standards of Artisan ingredients, brewing methods, and ownership. See also *Craft brewery*.

**mouthfeel**   How the beer feels in the mouth. It might be full or thin; dry, bitter, or sweet; smooth or creamy.

**Munchener Helles**   A Lager that is lighter in color, with a spicy bitterness complementing the malty sweetness.

**near beer**   Classified as a malt beverage, it contains less than 0.5 percent alcohol and was brewed particularly during Prohibition, thus enabling some breweries to stay in operation. Most popular during Prohibition were Bevo from Anheuser-Busch, Famo from Schlitz, Pablo from Pabst, and Vivo from Miller.

**nose (or bouquet)**   Terms used to describe a beer's fragrance or aroma. A beer's aroma or odor can be classified as (1) smelling of hops ("hoppy"); (2) smelling of malt ("malty"); and (3) smelling of nuts ("nutty"), spices ("spicy"), or fruit ("fruity"). If it smells like sulphur or chlorine, the beer should not be used.

**Oktoberfest**   A malt-centric style of Lager. The Oktoberfest celebration takes place over two weeks during late September and early October in Munich, Germany, where it originated in 1810. It has become a worldwide festival where this unique malt-centric Lager is served.

**on nitro (or nitrogenated)**   These beers have a smoother mouth-feel; a denser, longer-lasting head; and more prominent lacing on the glassware because the bubbles are smaller than in beers that have only oxygen. Nitrogen is infused through mechanical means for beers on draft and in cans.

**pasteurization**   A process to kill bacteria; for beer, to stop the growth of yeast. It usually involves spraying bottled or canned beer at the end of the bottling line for 2 or 3 minutes with very hot water, at least 140°F.

**Pilsner**   A golden-colored, dry, carbonated style of Lager attributed to the Bohemian town of Pilsen (now in the Czech Republic). Mass-market, Pilsner-style beers in the United States are brewed to be less sharp, crisp, and invigoratingly bitter than the original Pilsners. Artisan Pilsners are now brewed closer to the original ingredients and brewing methods.

**plug**   See *bung*.

**Porter (or London Porter)**   A well-hopped brown beer made from brown malt; a dark and full-bodied Ale. Named to honor the London street and river porters who most enjoyed this style of beer. An unproven story is that it was "invented" in eighteenth-century London by brewers who blended three different types of beer popular at the time.

**pub**   Short for a "public house," which originated in England, where it served as the center of a community. People gathered to converse, play games, have a pint and a meal, read the local paper, carry on business, and engage in a weekly "quiz" that covered a range of topics. If a person could not afford an office, the "pub" was the logical meeting place. Pubs must have a license to serve alcoholic beverages.

**publican**   The owner or manager of a pub in England and Ireland; equivalent to the bartender in the United States, though some brew-pub owners identify themselves as publicans.

**racking (or rack)**   Putting beers into casks or kegs; transferring beer from one vessel to another vessel, which is done to leave unwanted sediment behind.

**Rauchbier**   In German, *rauch* is smoke; this beer recipe requires a portion of the malt to be beechwood smoked in the kilning process.

**regional Craft brewery**   See *Craft brewery*.

**Reinheitsgebot**   The German Purity Law that allows only water, malted barley, malted wheat, hops, and yeast as ingredients in the brewing of beer.

**serving temperature**   Over-chilled Artisan beers need to be warmed before drinking, to allow enjoyment of all the flavors and aromas. Mass-produced beers are specially served very cold because they lack layers of flavors and aromas and taste best when ice cold. Artisan Pale Ales, along with Amber and Dark Lagers, are best served between 50°F and 55°F. Pale Lagers, such as Artisan Pilsners, should be served between 45°F and 50°F. Artisan Dark Ales and Stouts are best between 55°F and 60°F. Beer in Britain is served at cellar temperature, which is between 52°F and 60°F.

**shelf life**   Pasteurized beer is considered fresh and drinkable for 120 days from bottling or canning. Nonpasteurized beers have a shelf life of 60 days.

**skunky**   Any kind of light creates a chemical reaction in beer that resembles the smell of a skunk's spray. While brown bottles protect a beer's quality better than green or clear bottles, beer in any bottle should be stored away from any kind of light.

**small beer**   Brewed in colonial America for household use, it contains very little alcohol but all the nutrition and safety of a regular beer, because it is brewed under the same standards of boiling the water and malt for wort. It was used to provide liquid nourishment along with the healthful qualities natural to malted grains. Malted milk products became a substitute in later times and spiked in sales during U.S. Prohibition.

**sparge**   The process of recovering the residual sugar by rinsing the grain bed in the lauter tun with hot water.

**spent grains**   The solid residue separated from the mash. Local farmers typically pick up spent grain from the brewery to feed livestock and for use in gardens. Bakers use spent grains to make bread.

**spices**   Added to beer in the brewing process to enhance flavors. Orange peel and coriander are part of the Belgian Wheat recipe. However, yeast is the reason for spice aromas and taste in most beers.

**Stout**   The term given to the strongest Porters—thus, at 7 to 8 percent, they are referred to as "Stoutest" Porters. There are Dark Hued and Blonde Stouts. Variations include Dry Stout, Imperial Stout, and Baltic Porter. See also *English Stout* and *Irish Stout*.

**strength**   A general term for the amount of alcohol present in a beer.

**style**   A beer that has certain discernible characteristics, specific ingredients, and brewing method constitutes a style. Some styles have substyles; see also *Wheat beer*, with its substyles.

**Trappist Ale**   While both Abbey Ales and Trappist Ales are similar in taste profile as strong, fruity, and earthy, Trappist Ales are distinguished as being brewed in one of seven existing Trappist monastic breweries; six are located in Belgium, and one in is the Netherlands. All profits from Trappist Ales must be used for charitable purposes.

**Weissbier (or Weisse)**   A Wheat beer from Bavaria, in southern Germany; *weisse* is German for "white."

**Weizenbier (or Weizen)**   A Wheat beer; *weizen* is German for "wheat."

**Weizenbock**   A strong Wheat beer made in the German Bock style, fermented with a special yeast that gives a spicy clovelike flavor.

**Wheat beer**   German purity laws require brewing Wheat beers mainly with wheat. There are slight variations in the recipe and different names for Wheat beer, according to location, recipe, and brewing method. See the various styles *Weissbier, Weizenbier, Hefeweissbier, Kristallweissbier, Dunkles Weissbier, Weizenbock, Witbier,* and *La Bière Blanche.*

**wild yeast**   Yeast that naturally exists in the environment.

**Witbier (or Wit)**   The Dutch name for the Belgian style of Wheat beer. See also *Belgian Wheat beer.*

**wort**   The liquid sugar solution separated from the heated malt and water. It becomes the body of the beer.

**yeast**   A single-celled microorganism that thrives on sugar, which it ferments. Yeast is essential in the brewing process. Different strains of yeast impart different aromas and flavors to beer. Special beer yeasts are developed in laboratories dedicated to the Craft/Artisan beer industry. See also *fermentation.*

**zymurgy**   Originating with Louis Pasteur's laboratory work concerning yeast and fermentation, and thus confined to the science of fermentation, zymurgy has become a generic term to describe the process of brewing beer.

# Resources

There is a growing body of up-to-the-minute information about Craft beers to keep pace with the daily industry growth. Most magazines and journals are available in libraries and in stores where Craft beer is sold. Some brewpubs have a magazine rack for browsing. Craft beer bloggers are proliferating worldwide. Have fun seeking and finding everything new.

## Beer-Themed Magazines and Newspapers

*Ale Street News* (newspaper)
Industry news, regional news, opinions, and travel for beer.
www.alestreetnews.com

*All About Beer Magazine*
"Celebrating the world of beer culture," with reviews and the latest beer news.
http://allaboutbeer.com

*Beer Advocate Magazine*
"Beer talk" on all topics worldwide.
http://beeradvocate.com

*The Beer Connoisseur*
The international beer scene—a fine beer and food section with complimentary and contrasting selections.
www.beerconnoisseur.com/Beer-Magazine

*Beer West Magazine*
Emphasis on West Coast events and brews.
www.beerwestmag.com

*Brew Your Own*
The how-to homebrew magazine.
www.byo.com

*Brewing News* (newspaper)
Each region has its own newspaper with specific state news and
general regional articles.
www.brewingnews.com

*Celebrator Beer News Magazine*
Coverage of events on the West Coast, international beer stories,
and the beer industry.
www.celebrator.com

*Draft Magazine*
Features that include a monthly "beer town" close-up, with events
and brewer profiles.
http://draftmag.com

*Modern Brewery Age*
The business magazine for the beer industry; includes interviews
with brewers, legal data, and ideas for sales.
www.breweryage.com

*Yankee Brew News*
Specifically for New England, with a state column.
www.brewingnews.com/yankeebrew

*Zymurgy*
Official magazine of the American Homebrewers Association (AHA).
www.homebrewersassociation.org/pages/zymurgy/
about-the-magazine

# Beer Blogs and Websites

http://beerbloggersconference.org/blogs/complete-list-of-beer-blogs
Information on the annual July beer bloggers conferences in the
United States and UK.

http://beeradvocate.com
International news, personalities, events, and reviews.

www.ratebeer.com
Consumer-driven reviews on beers and breweries throughout the
world.

www.craftbeer.com
Information on the business of brewing, with worldwide news, com-
mentaries, events, profiles, and education; maintained by the Brewers
Association.

www.homebrewtalk.com
Homebrew forums and assistance, with recipes and product reviews.

www.brewersassociation.org
Brewing industry news.

http://beerfestivals.org
Annual list of worldwide festivals, organized by month.

www.greatamericanbeerfestival.com
Information on the annual October event in Denver, Colorado.
Breweries worldwide compete for top honors (gold, silver, and bronze
medals) in more than 100 styles.

www.craftbeer.com/news-and-events/all-beer-weeks
U.S. Craft beer weeks, listed by city, state, and region.

www.craftbeer.com/news-and-events/american-craft-beer-week
The specifics on how to participate in this annual May event.

http://brookstonbeerbulletin.com/beer-weeks
A list of U.S. and worldwide Craft beer weeks and beer holidays.
Overall an excellent website for the fun aspects of Craft beer, with
mentions of brewers' birthdays and highlights of beer art.

# Titles of Lasting Interest

British author Michael Jackson remains the ultimate authority on
Craft beer in its historical and modern context. Some of his most
popular titles include these:

- *Ultimate Beer* (Dorling Kindersley Limited, 1998)
  Offers an introduction to beers worldwide.

- *Michael Jackson's Great Beers of Belgium* (Brewers Publications,
  2008)
  Gives a detailed account of Belgian beers, from earliest to
  modern times.

- *Michael Jackson's Beer Companion: Revised and Updated*
  (Courage Books, 2007)
  Covers the world's great beer styles, gastronomy, and
  traditions.

- *Great Beer Guide* (Barnes & Noble, 2006)
  Describes 500 worldwide classic brews.

- *The New World Guide to Beer* (Prentice Hall, 1997)
  Discusses beers of all the nations.

Garrett Oliver has become the U.S. spokesperson for beer, consumed
both at home and when eating out. Some of his titles include these:

- *The Brewmaster's Table: Discovering the Pleasures of Real Beer
  with Real Food* (Ecco, 2005)
  Reveals why beer is the perfect beverage with food at any
  meal.

- *The Oxford Companion to Beer* (Oxford University Press, 2011) All about beer, by experts who define it within the context of history and culture.

Lucy Saunders offers tips and ideas from renowned chefs in brew-pubs and restaurants. Saunders is also the editor of www.beercook. com. Some of her titles include these:

- *The Best of American Beer and Food: Pairing and Cooking with Craft Beer* (Brewers Publications, 2007)

- *Grilling with Beer: Bastes, BBQ Sauces, Mops, Marinades & More Made with Craft Beer* (F & B Communications, 2009)

- *Cooking with Beer: Taste-Tempting Recipes and Creative Ideas for Matching Beer & Food* (Time Life Education, 1996)

Tom Standage's *A History of the World in 6 Glasses* (Walker Publishing Company, 2006) is one of the best books about what we drink and why. It helps you understand how culture, politics, and economics influence what we drink.

# Beyond the Brewery

Beer museums are found all over the world. I've listed a few here, according to county, to whet your interest in taking time out to tour a museum as you travel. Of course, seek out others and keep track of them to share with family and friends—and let us know, too, so that we can add your recommendations in future editions. Send your suggestions to rkohn@nuvo.net.

## Belgium

A visit to Belgium provides you with no fewer than 23 options, including 2 in Antwerp, 3 in Brussels, 3 in Namur, and 5 in West Flanders. The following website lists them all: www.upfront-live. com/gg/index.php?option=com_weblinks&view=category&id= 44&Itemid=1121.

The Hops Museum in Poperinge might be the most intriguing. The Brewers' House on the Grand Place in Brussels can occupy you for at least two hours as you explore brewing methods from medieval times to the present. The Musée Bruxellois de la Gueuze is part of the Cantillon Brewery (near the Midi train station at Rue Ghedye 56). Here you can experience a working brewery and taste the distinctive gueuze. Don't overlook the museum dedicated to brewery trucks in Namur, a short distance from Brussels.

If you're making a trip to Belgium, which is about the size of the state of Maryland and has around 100 breweries, plan accordingly so you can more fully enjoy your brewery tours.

## The Netherlands

In Amsterdam, it's touted as "the Heineken Experience" (a.k.a. Museum). Established in 1864, within walking distance of the Rijksmuseum, the original brewery closed in 1988 and was converted into an immersion of the brewing process and the industry as a whole.

Alkmaar, just outside Amsterdam, is considered the cheese capital of Holland. It hosts the Holland Cheese Museum, along with National Beer Museum De Boom. Together they make for an engrossing experience. The museum is in the brewery, founded in the seventeenth century, and offers a glimpse into the "old ways" of brewing. Then go to the cellar, where the "pub" offers tastes of 86 currently brewed Dutch beers.

## Germany

State-of-the-art beer museums are part of beer gardens and breweries, as well as stand-alone museums in the center of towns and cities. If you're heading to Germany for Oktoberfest, it's worth a visit to Kulmbach to visit the Kulmbacher Mönchshof. Hands-on exhibits explore the brewing industry from the farm to the glass in your hand, beer culture through the centuries, beer advertising, and brewery construction. Nearby is the Mönchshof-Bräuhaus restaurant, where you can sample Kulmbacher beers along with compatible foods. For more information, check out www.bayerisches-brauereimuseum.de.

## Austria

If you're going to Salzburg for the Mozart Festival, plan to spend a leisurely visit at Stiegl Brauwelt, where you can get caught up in the most minute details of how to enjoy beer. The Brewery, which has been in operation since 1492, sources its spring water from Untersberg mountain. It's fun to conjecture whether Mozart might have been enjoying the very same brews.

## Czech Republic

In Pilsen, the Brewery Museum emphasizes the ongoing cultural history of beer, dating back to Egypt. This museum shows all aspects of the beer-making process, including a mating operation. If you purchase a souvenir glass, you get a taste of Pilsner Urquell, made from the original recipe.

## Ireland

A visit to Dublin is complete only with a stop at Guinness Storehouse. Since 1759, the harp symbol has been the essence of establishing a global brand. Throughout seven floors, the brewing story unfolds, and you're in the midst of the tradition (including cooking with Stout). Sampling the traditional recipes is a special treat and inspires you to go home and cook with beer (both in your hand and in the pot!).

## United States

Pottsville, Pennsylvania, is the home of Yuengling Brewery, the oldest continuously operating U.S. brewery. Founded in 1829, it offers a guided tour through the old brewhouse and shows you the caves where the beer was stored before it was moved to the refrigeration units. The visit includes an ornate bar in the taproom, where you can taste their full-flavored beer that's been around for 190 years, despite Prohibition and the advent of light Lagers.

# Finding the Beer You Want to Drink

Not all import and U.S. Craft beers are available nationally. Currently, only Samuel Adams, Sierra Nevada, and Rogue Brewing are available in all 50 U.S. states. About 15,000 U.S. brands come from about 1,000 production brewers, and about another 1,500 brewpubs' brands are available regionally or within a specific state, county, or city.

Distributors of import beers tend to distribute import beers regionally. If you can't find what you want at your local bottle shop (even after asking whether they can get it for you), try checking the brewery website either by name of the brewery or by the brand name. If that doesn't get you the desired result, check out the online "Beer Man" to learn where a brew is generally distributed:

www.postcrescent.com/section/APC0402/APC-Beer-Man

You can contact "Beer Man" columnist Todd Haefer at beerman@postcrescent.com. The "Beer Man" column provides a weekly profile of beers from across the United States and worldwide.

# Tasting Sheets

Keeping a journal of beers you drink is an essential way to keep track of what, where, and when you have sampled a brew. It is a prompt for your memory as well as a reference to go back when someone asks for a recommendation. Place the sheets in any order that makes sense to you—by style or brand of beer, location, or date. A loose leaf binder with tabs works well for storage, and the loose sheets are easy to carry with you when you go to tasting events away from home.

# "In Good Taste" Tasting Sheets

**Date of Event:** _____

**Place of Event:** _____

**Beer Style Name:** _____

**Style Characteristics to Look For:** (BJCP synopsis) _____

_____

_____

_____

**Brand Name #1**: (Closest to Judging Style) _____

Aroma: _____

_____

Appearance: _____

_____

Flavor: _____

_____

Body: _____

_____

Finish/Aftertaste: _____

_____

Overall Impression: _____

_____

_____

What I particularly learned during the conversation: _____

_____

_____

Which of the other samples seems closest to the style? _____

_____

_____

Which beer did I personally best like/enjoy? _____

_____

Why? _____

_____

**Brand Name #2**: _____

Aroma: _____

_____

Appearance: _____

_____

Flavor: _____

_____

Body: _____

_____

Finish/Aftertaste: _____

_____

Overall Impression: _____

_____

_____

What I particularly learned during the conversation: _____

_____

_____

Which of the other samples seems closest to the style? _____

_____

_____

Which beer did I personally best like/enjoy? _____

_____

Why? _____

_____

**Brand Name #3**: _____

Aroma: _____

_____

Appearance: _____

_____

Flavor: _____

_____

Body: _____

_____

Finish/Aftertaste: _____

_____

Overall Impression: _____

_____

_____

What I particularly learned during the conversation: _____

_____

_____

Which of the other samples seems closest to the style? _____

_____

_____

Which beer did I personally best like/enjoy? _____

_____

Why? _____

_____

**Brand Name #4:** _____

Aroma: _____
_____

Appearance: _____
_____

Flavor: _____
_____

Body: _____
_____

Finish/Aftertaste: _____
_____

Overall Impression: _____
_____
_____

What I particularly learned during the conversation: _____
_____
_____

Which of the other samples seems closest to the style? _____
_____
_____

Which beer did I personally best like/enjoy? _____
_____

Why? _____
_____

**Brand Name #5**: _____

Aroma: _____
_____

Appearance: _____
_____

Flavor: _____
_____

Body: _____
_____

Finish/Aftertaste: _____
_____

Overall Impression: _____
_____
_____

What I particularly learned during the conversation: _____
_____
_____

Which of the other samples seems closest to the style? _____
_____
_____

Which beer did I personally best like/enjoy? _____
_____

Why? _____
_____

# "Mix 'n' Match" Tasting Sheets

Date of Event: _____

Place of Event: _____

Featured Food: _____

Specific Taste Profile of the Featured Food: _____

_____

**Featured Beer #1 Brand/Style**: _____

Specific taste profile of this beer: _____

_____

_____

What I particularly like about this combination: _____

_____

_____

_____

What I do not like about this combination: _____

_____

_____

_____

**Featured Beer #2 Brand/Style**: _____

Specific taste profile of this beer: _____

_____

_____

What I particularly like about this combination: _____

_____

_____

_____

What I do not like about this combination: _____

_____

_____

**Featured Beer #3 Brand/Style:** _____

Specific taste profile of this beer: _____

_____

_____

What I particularly like about this combination: _____

_____

_____

_____

What I do not like about this combination: _____

_____

_____

_____

**Featured Beer #4 Brand/Style:** _____

Specific taste profile of this beer: _____

_____

_____

What I particularly like about this combination: _____

_____

_____

_____

What I do not like about this combination: _____

_____

_____

_____

# "Great Traditions" Tasting Sheets

**Date of Event:** _____

**Place of Event:** _____

**Beer Tradition From:** _____

_____

_____

**Featured Beer Brand and Style:** _____

_____

_____

Aroma: _____

_____

Appearance: _____

_____

Flavor: _____

_____

Body: _____

_____

Finish/Aftertaste: _____

_____

Overall Impression: _____

_____

_____

**U.S.-Made Beer #1 Brand Name in the Style of:** _____

_____

_____

Aroma: _____

_____

Appearance: _____

_____

Flavor: _____

_____

Body: _____

_____

Finish/Aftertaste: _____

_____

Overall Impression: _____

_____

_____

## U.S.-Made Beer #2 Brand Name in the Style of: _____

_____

_____

Aroma: _____

_____

Appearance: _____

_____

Flavor: _____

_____

Body: _____

_____

Finish/Aftertaste: _____

_____

Overall Impression: _____

_____

_____

## U.S.-Made Beer #3 Brand Name in the Style of: _____

_____

_____

Aroma: _____

_____

Appearance: _____

_____

Flavor: _____

_____

Body: _____

_____

Finish/Aftertaste: _____

_____

Overall Impression: _____

_____

_____

# "Beers by Season" Tasting Sheets

**Date of Event:** _____

**Place of Event:** _____

**Beer Season:** _____

**Brand Name #1**: _____

What is distinctive about this beer that makes it appropriate for the season? Is it seasonally sourced products as part of the recipe, alcohol strength, flavor?

_____

_____

_____

Aroma: _____

_____

Appearance: _____

_____

Flavor: _____

_____

Body: _____

_____

Finish/Aftertaste: _____

_____

Overall Impression: _____

_____

_____

As you enjoy a variety of seasonal brews, comment on which pleases you the most and the least. What qualities are most pleasing?

_____

_____

**Brand Name #2**: _____

What is distinctive about this beer that makes it appropriate for the season? Is it seasonally sourced products as part of the recipe, alcohol strength, flavor?

_____

_____

_____

Aroma: _____

_____

Appearance: _____

_____

Flavor: _____

_____

Body: _____

_____

Finish/Aftertaste: _____

_____

Overall Impression: _____

_____

_____

As you enjoy a variety of seasonal brews, comment on which pleases you the most and the least. What qualities are most pleasing?

_____

_____

**Brand Name #3**: _____

What is distinctive about this beer that makes it appropriate for the season? Is it seasonally sourced products as part of the recipe, alcohol strength, flavor?

_____

_____

_____

Aroma: _____

_____

Appearance: _____

_____

Flavor: _____

_____

Body: _____

_____

Finish/Aftertaste: _____

_____

Overall Impression: _____

_____

_____

As you enjoy a variety of seasonal brews, comment on which pleases you the most and the least. What qualities are most pleasing?

_____

_____

**Brand Name #4**: _____

What is distinctive about this beer that makes it appropriate for the season? Is it seasonally sourced products as part of the recipe, alcohol strength, flavor?

_____

_____

_____

Aroma: _____

_____

Appearance: _____

_____

Flavor: _____

_____

Body: _____

_____

Finish/Aftertaste: _____

_____

Overall Impression: _____

_____

_____

As you enjoy a variety of seasonal brews, comment on which pleases you the most and the least. What qualities are most pleasing?

_____

_____

# Index

heat, beer pairings, 179
heated sugars, adding, 64
Hefeweizen, 92, 94, 108
  head, 122
herbs
  adding, 63
  beer pairings, 179
Herodotus, 7
Herrera, Gabriel Alonso de, 16
Herz, Julia, 42
High Falls Brewing Company, 43
*Histories*, 7
Holloway, Thomas, 20
Holsten Pils, 147
*Home Brewer's Companion*, 11
homebrewing, 27-28
homebrew supply stores, tastings, 118
honey wine. *See* mead
hopbacks, 75
hoppiness versus maltiness, 125-128
hops, 8, 19, 57-58, 126-127
  aromatic, 58
  finding, 59-60
  food pairings, 179
hosting tastings, 183-185, 195-196
  guests
    knowledge, 185-186
    preparing, 186-189
  provisions, 187-188
  themes, 189-190, 194
    Beers by Season, 194
    Great Traditions, 193-194
    In Good Taste, 191-192
    Mix 'n' Match, 192-193

**I**

IBU (international bittering unit), 65-66
Imperial Stouts, food pairings, 181
InBev, 33
India Pale Ales (IPAs), 82
  American Style, 107
  food pairings, 181
Intercourse Brewing Company, 38
international bittering unit (IBU), 65-66
IPAs (India Pale Ales), 82
  American Style, 107
  food pairings, 181
Irish imperial pints, 170
Irish Red Ales, 104

**J**

Jackalope Brewing Company, 39
Jackson, Michael, 16, 37, 60, 80, 85, 96, 102
Jacobsen, J. C., 61
Jefferson, Martha, 20
Jefferson, Thomas, 20-22
Jolly Pumpkin Artisan Ales, 111
Jordan, Kim, 38
Joseph Schlitz Brewing Company, 21, 26, 35
journals, tasting, 129-130

**K**

*Kalevla*, 9
Kassendorf Amphora, 91
kelches, 171
Kirin Brewery Company, 11-12

# U–V

# W

# X-Y-Z